I'd like to put this book in [the hands of every woman who has] experienced the trauma of discovering that her [husband is addicted] to pornography. Reading *Aftershock* is like sitting down with empathetic counselors who offer a roadmap to recovery.

    GARY CHAPMAN, PHD, author of *The 5 Love Languages*

Aftershock is a hands-on, biblically grounded resource that will guide you toward hope and healing. From their expertise and many years of experience, Joann and Geremy provide compassionate and practical advice to address the real-life questions and experiences you are facing. This book will remind you that you are not alone!

    DR. JULI SLATTERY, clinical psychologist; author of *Rethinking Sexuality: God's Design and Why It Matters*; president of Authentic Intimacy

I'm always excited when another quality book rises up to offer hope, tools, and healing to women devastated by betrayal. When a woman faces the devastation of a cheating husband, there is no such thing as too many resources. She will need to hear other women's stories of hope, she will need to understand the forensics of sexual addiction, and she will need wise godly counsel. Joann and Geremy provide this through their book *Aftershock*. The voices are honest, hopeful, and full of biblical wisdom. This is a must-read for any Christian woman's healing library.

    MEG WILSON, founder of Hope After Betrayal Ministries and author of *Hope After Betrayal: Healing When Sexual Addiction Invades Your Marriage*

This book is absolutely crucial for a woman to read as she walks through recovery from her husband's issues with pornography or sexual infidelity. Far too few resources exist for this problem that is plaguing countless marriages across the country and around the world. When a wife finds herself reeling from the impact of her husband's choices, she needs sound, trustworthy, biblically based advice. *Aftershock* can be that trusted voice in your journey. This is not a path that any one of us can navigate alone. This invaluable resource can gently guide you into how to face your emotions, construct a plan to work with your husband, and find hope to stay the course as you go through the ups and downs of recovery. We wish this book had been available when we walked through a restoration process over a decade ago. We learned many of these exact same insights from expert counselors and teachers. But *Aftershock* packs all of that wisdom into one powerful "roadmap" for your recovery. We highly recommend this book for anyone facing the tumultuous journey from loss and betrayal to hope, healing, and freedom. There is joy on the other side!

NICK AND MICHELLE STUMBO, Pure Desire Ministries

With dozens of captivating anecdotes, practical advice, and sound integration of theology and psychology, *Aftershock* offers help and hope to wives deluged by their husbands' secret sins. Condie and Keeton guide you through the ups and downs of a personal recovery that offers your marriage the best opportunity for reconciliation. This is the book I've been needing for over two decades, to use in my own practice specializing in the treatment of sex addiction.

ROB JACKSON, MS, LPC, certified clinical sex addiction specialist

I'm excited *Aftershock* is available. I personally know the authors, and for years, I've followed their work in the area of marriages struggling with pornography or other sexual addictions. *Aftershock* does not give an empty guarantee to the reader that everything will be "happy ever after." What it does provide is a balanced, honest, straightforward explanation of the problem and a practical, doable plan—a plan that helps the reader see the problem clearly, confront her husband, and recognize what true, long-lasting recovery looks like. If you find yourself reeling in the aftershock of discovering your husband's pornography addiction or affair, I would highly suggest you read this book before doing anything else.

    TIM SANFORD, licensed professional counselor and author of several books, including *Forgive for Real: Six Steps to Forgiving*

Women who discover their husbands are involved in pornography experience a myriad of emotions—from shock to anger to heartache to a deep sense of betrayal and loss. Joann Condie and Geremy Keeton have a wealth of counseling experience in this arena, and they have written *Aftershock* as a means of providing wives with concrete steps they can take and offering them renewed hope for the future. If you or someone you know is facing the pain of a spouse's pornography addiction, we highly recommend this book.

    DR. GREG AND ERIN SMALLEY, Focus on the Family Marriage and Family Formation; coauthors of *Reconnected: Moving from Roommates to Soulmates in Your Marriage*

If you've discovered that your husband has become involved in pornography, you're likely feeling heartbroken, confused, and desperate for help. Know that you're not alone—Joann Condie has counseled many other women who have walked through similar crises, and she can help you navigate this painful season as well. *Aftershock* offers tangible, biblically based steps you can take to move toward healing and hope.

    JIM DALY, president, Focus on the Family

I have the utmost respect and admiration for Joann and Geremy. Their expertise in counseling and personal care for a wife facing sexual betrayal is evident on every page. The content in this book is powerful for helping a wife discover hope and healing after sexual infidelity has been disclosed. For wives wanting personal and practical help in navigating the recovery process after betrayal, *Aftershock* is a must-have resource. You won't regret following the advice in this book!

    JONATHAN DAUGHERTY, founder and president, Be Broken Ministries

Aftershock . . . is a great resource for women. The book offers a clear, wise, compassionate, and biblical approach for healing and restoration. I highly recommend this book for hurting wives and the counselors who are committed to assisting them on their recovery journey.

    DR. JOHN THORINGTON, counselor and author of *Pure Teens: Honoring God, Relationships, and Sex* and *Pure Teens: Free to Love*

In *Aftershock*, Joann Condie and Geremy Keeton calm the chaos of sexually betrayed women with expert spiritual support and an immensely compassionate bedside manner. Their decades of counseling couples through marital crisis is evident on every page through practical, methodical, and deeply spiritual guidance for walking forward through pain and into lasting healing. This book is essential reading not only for wounded wives, but for any caregiver pastors, counselors, small group leaders, or friends who choose to walk with women through one of life's most painful challenges.

    DANIEL WEISS, president of the Brushfires Foundation

AFTERSHOCK

AFTER

Overcoming His Secret Life with Pornography

SHOCK

A Plan for Recovery

JOANN CONDIE
with Geremy Keeton

FOCUS ON THE FAMILY.
A Focus on the Family Resource
Published by Tyndale House Publishers

Aftershock: Overcoming His Secret Life with Pornography: A Plan for Recovery
© 2020 Focus on the Family. All rights reserved.

A Focus on the Family book published by Tyndale House Publishers, Carol Stream, Illinois 60188

Focus on the Family and the accompanying logo and design are federally registered trademarks of Focus on the Family, 8605 Explorer Drive, Colorado Springs, CO 80920.

TYNDALE and Tyndale's quill logo are registered trademarks of Tyndale House Publishers.

No part of this publication may be reproduced, stored in a retrieval system, or transmitted in any form or by any means—electronic, mechanical, photocopy, recording, or otherwise—without prior written permission of Focus on the Family.

All Scripture quotations, unless otherwise marked, are from *The Holy Bible, English Standard Version*. Copyright © 2001 by CrosswayBibles, a publishing ministry of Good News Publishers. Used by permission. All rights reserved. Scripture quotations marked MSG are taken from *THE MESSAGE*, copyright © 1993, 2002, 2018 by Eugene H. Peterson. Used by permission of NavPress. All rights reserved. Represented by Tyndale House Publishers. Scripture quotations marked (NIV) are taken from the *Holy Bible, New International Version*®, *NIV*®. Copyright © 1973, 1978, 1984, 2011 by Biblica, Inc.® Used by permission of Zondervan. All rights reserved worldwide. (*www.zondervan.com*) The "NIV" and "New International Version" are trademarks registered in the United States Patent and Trademark Office by Biblica, Inc®. Scripture quotations marked (NKJV) are taken from the *New King James Version*®. Copyright © 1982 by Thomas Nelson. Used by permission. All rights reserved.

Cover illustration of storm texture copyright © Eclectic Anthology/Design Cuts. All rights reserved.

Cover design by Julie Chen. Interior design by Eva M. Winters.

The case examples presented in this book are fictional composites based on the authors' clinical experience with hundreds of clients through the years. Any resemblance between these fictional characters and actual persons is coincidental.

The use of material from or references to various websites does not imply endorsement of those sites in their entirety. Availability of websites and pages is subject to change without notice.

For information about special discounts for bulk purchases, please contact Tyndale House Publishers at csresponse@tyndale.com, or call 1-800-323-9400.

Library of Congress Cataloging-in-Publication Data

Names: Condie, Joann, author.
Title: Aftershock : overcoming his secret life with pornography: a plan for recovery / Joann Condie ; with Geremy Keeton.
Description: Carol Stream, Illinois : Tyndale House Publishers, [2020] |
Identifiers: LCCN 2020016880 (print) | LCCN 2020016881 (ebook) | ISBN 9781589976979 (cloth) | ISBN 9781684282944 (ebook) | ISBN 9781684282951 (epub) | ISBN 9781684282968 (kindle edition)
Subjects: LCSH: Husbands—Sexual behavior. | Wives—Religious life. | Pornography—Religious aspects. | Women—Psychology.
Classification: LCC HQ28 .C66 2020 (print) | LCC HQ28 (ebook) | DDC 306.872/2—dc23
LC record available at https://lccn.loc.gov/2020016880
LC ebook record available at https://lccn.loc.gov/2020016881

Printed in the United States of America

26 25 24 23 22 21
7   6   5   4   3   2

We dedicate this book to the many wives and couples who have taught us so much by their brave and God-reliant approach to recovery and the surrender to Him it takes. The Lord is good and faithful in all times and in all circumstances.
—*Joann and Geremy*

CONTENTS

Introduction *1*

CHAPTER 1 Aftershock *7*
CHAPTER 2 "Can I Trust My Emotions?" *25*
CHAPTER 3 "What Was I Thinking?" *47*
CHAPTER 4 Take Care of Yourself *59*
CHAPTER 5 "Why Does He Do What He Does?" *77*
CHAPTER 6 Making Decisions and Preparing for Action *97*
CHAPTER 7 Confronting Your Husband *117*
CHAPTER 8 The Road to Recovery *137*
CHAPTER 9 Your Sexual Relationship with Your Husband *163*
CHAPTER 10 Setting Yourself Up for Success *181*

Acknowledgments *199*
Appendix A: Sleep Tips *201*
Appendix B: A Man's Invitation to Recovery *207*
Notes *211*

INTRODUCTION

YOU'VE PICKED UP THIS BOOK because something happened or has been happening for a long time: Your husband has used pornography, and that may, or may not, have led to other unfaithful actions.

I'm sorry. *So very sorry.* Whatever the details are in your situation, I'm certain it hasn't been easy, and you'd much rather be reaching for some other kind of reading material. But you've picked up *this* book. The "something" you now live with shocks you and leaves you swirling as you face a reality you never anticipated being part of your marriage.

You may feel as if your inner world is crumbling in the aftershock of this devastating betrayal. Maybe on the surface you're holding the threads of your life together for the sake of your family. But those threads are fraying, and the painful reality of your situation feels overwhelming.

There Is Hope

The crisis you're experiencing is real. Pornography use is widespread and damaging. The fallout often includes broken relationships and failed marriages.

But hang on! Hope lives and is available to you and your husband.

I have had the humbling honor of watching as people's lives and marriages are restored against all odds—even in worst-case scenarios—so I have confidence for you as well. I believe and trust that God will begin a transformation in you beyond anything you've ever imagined or thought possible. I also believe that your spouse can experience such a transformation, depending on his choices.

I've counseled many women, men, and couples who have struggled with the damage that pornography use has caused. These hurting people often begin counseling with little to no hope that the process will heal and restore their broken marriages. But they agree, sometimes out of desperation, to keep walking toward restoration with me and with the God who loves them and wants them to enjoy the blessings of a faithful marriage.

I passionately desire to reach out to you through the pages of this book and infuse you with hope. You are not alone! I do understand, and I do believe in you. I believe that you can get through this crisis and look back in amazement at the transformation that has taken place in your whole being.

There is no quick fix for what has happened. As you walk this path toward recovery, you'll experience times of discouragement when you'll be tempted to put this book on the shelf and give up. The process I explain in this book will take commitment on your part. It's true that you'll only get out of this process what you put into it. But the value of your work will be immeasurable!

The Goal of This Book

Aftershock is for women whose husbands struggle with pornography and other actions along the spectrum of sexual sin, including physical infidelity. Although there are admittedly some differences between pornography use alone versus a complete "real-life" physical affair*, when it comes to the psychological impact and effects on a wife, they are often virtually identical. So, for the purposes of this book, we will refer to each scenario similarly due to the overlapping emotional damage and general steps of recovery that they share. Every word of this book is designed to help you heal, grow, and recover. This book is about you and your journey, but it will also impact your spouse and your marriage. If you commit to the process I describe, you will change, your relationship with your husband will change, and your marriage will change.

It is my sincere prayer that you, your husband, and your marriage will improve dramatically. But you can only control yourself. My focus is on you! You are not the cause of your husband's poor choices, and you desperately need to believe this fact. The information in this book can certainly help your husband change, heal, and grow, but please make your own needs and well-being a priority on this journey. Helping yourself is key to helping your marriage.

---

* For remarks about the question of divorce in the face of pornography use alone, see Focus on the Family's question-and-answer "Pornography as Grounds for Divorce?" at focusonthefamily.com/family-qa/pornography-as-grounds-for-divorce/.

Helpful Tools

At the end of each chapter, you'll find a reflection, questions to answer, and a prayer. These tools are designed to help you absorb the material you've read so you can receive the most benefit from this book.

After reading the reflection, think about it for a moment and then write down your thoughts and feelings. Writing in a personal journal is a great place to start. It's generally more helpful to keep a physical journal than to make notes on a digital device. You could use any kind of notebook, but I suggest you buy a lovely blank book that makes you feel good just looking at it.

I recommend that you pray before writing in your journal. The reason is simple. Our loving God knows *everything* about you:

> O LORD, you have searched me and known me!
> You know when I sit down and when I rise up;
>   you discern my thoughts from afar.
> You search out my path and my lying down
>   and are acquainted with all my ways.
> Even before a word is on my tongue,
>   behold, O LORD, you know it altogether.
> PSALM 139:1-4

After praying and writing about the reflection, jot down in your journal your answers to the questions. Scientific studies have shown that it's helpful to record your thoughts and feelings, so make sure to answer these questions![1]

I've learned from experience that it can be difficult to

INTRODUCTION

describe your emotions when you're in crisis, so search on the internet for one of the many lists that describe emotions, such as a "feelings wheel" or "emotions chart." Print one that gives you many strong and descriptive words and refer to it often, especially at the end of each chapter as you get in touch with your heart. I hope you'll utilize this approach as you work through the questions for each chapter.

Writing in a journal is for *your* benefit. Your journal is a place to record not only your thoughts and feelings but also what you're praying and hoping for. Write down anything that helps you process your journey from pain to healing. Don't worry about how you write or what you say. Just be as honest with yourself as you can. This exercise can be very healing and freeing.

Finally, each chapter ends with a prayer. You may use the prepared prayers or your own words to ask for God's help.

The Authors

My coauthor, Geremy F. Keeton, and I developed the content for this book together, but each chapter is written in my voice. I'm a licensed professional counselor, as well as a registered nurse, and Geremy is a licensed marriage and family therapist with extensive experience in Christian ministry.

Geremy's devotion and expertise in helping men, especially with sexual recovery, has enhanced my work for numerous years. I'm highly aware that both partners in this painful situation need care and guidance. With that in mind, I asked Geremy for his insightful input to ensure that the concepts I present and the tone I use throughout the book are compatible with a man's recovery needs and emotional journey as well.

A Word from Geremy

Because my coauthorship is designed to go virtually unnoticed as Joann speaks to you directly, I want to take this opportunity to say hello and assure you that I care deeply about you and the journey you're on. I also want to echo Joann's confidence and hope that you can be restored to wholeness, and your marriage can not only be revived but can become all that God designed it to be.

My perspective as a male colleague working with Joann further shapes the book's tone and helps define specific man-motivating actions. This is *not* a book that bashes men. Joann and I want to help both you and your husband. But I'm also very aware that this book has been written to you, not your husband. You need compassion, care, and direction—yet we also hope that your recovery will ultimately help your husband, too.

You are not to blame for your husband's behavior or the pain it's causing you. No one "makes" another person act in unfaithful ways. This is not to say that your husband doesn't need compassion, care, and direction too. He does. But this is your time for healing.

My silent voice behind the words in the rest of this book reaches out too as Joann expresses what we both strongly believe. You can get through this. You are not alone. We value you, and the God who created you loves you more than words can express!

Where Are You Now?

Next, we'll talk about what *preshock*, *shock*, and *aftershock* mean and where you find yourself as you begin this process of restoration.

CHAPTER 1

AFTERSHOCK

*God gave us a spirit not of fear but of
power and love and self-control.*

2 TIMOTHY 1:7

AFTERSHOCK DESCRIBES YOUR REALITY after discovering your husband's pornography use or other sinful sexual behaviors. The marriage you thought you had has crumbled; shock consumes your thoughts and imagination; and you're grappling with how to live with the pain of betrayal soaking into every aspect of your life. You fear that more incidents of sexual unfaithfulness have happened, and more might happen in the future.

Dara's story illustrates her progression from preshock to shock and then to aftershock:

> The day Dara's son turned three, everyone gathered
> for his birthday party. Who could've wished for more?
> Friends, grandparents, and a smiling toddler bustled

around the house eating cake and singing "Happy Birthday." Timmy delighted in all the attention and the pile of presents waiting to be opened. Dara's husband, Geoff, even grilled a few steaks. The party was a super memory. The snapshots on Facebook proved it.

The following day, though, was a day of shock. "Happy Birthday" and steaks were yesterday. Anything normal in Dara's world was yesterday. This morning, Geoff accidentally left his phone behind when he left for work, and after a number of text messages came in, Dara decided to look at them in case she needed to call him. She didn't know his password, but she quickly guessed it.

When Dara saw the images and words on the screen, she realized that there was a lot she didn't know about her husband. She knew Geoff well enough to figure out his password, but apparently she didn't know him well enough to suspect what she was now staring at.

Dara looked at the screen in disbelief! Her heart raced as she saw a photo of a scantily clad woman in a provocative pose, with words beneath the image. It was evident that Geoff had found this woman online and had recently been sexting with her.

Dara sank into a kitchen chair. She was reeling. She couldn't move. She stared at the trappings of the birthday party that she'd been happily cleaning up only moments ago. *Did that party just happen yesterday?* she thought.

"I can't believe it," she said aloud. "I know he's been online a lot, especially late at night. But I trusted him.

I thought he was playing one of the games he seems so addicted to."

In desperation she called Geoff's office and tried to sound calm as she asked the receptionist for his extension. The sound of Geoff's voice mail rattled Dara. She couldn't handle leaving a message. Her hands shook as she laid her phone on the kitchen table.

What have I missed? she thought. *What does he get from this that he doesn't get from me? Aren't I enough for him? And this woman has his cell number! Do they talk to each other? Has he met her in person?*

Dara picked up her phone and called her next-door neighbor.

"Connie, something has come up, and I need to run an errand. Could Timmy stay with you for a little while?"

Connie agreed, and Dara managed a smile when she dropped Timmy off to play with Connie's daughter.

Dara drove to Geoff's office building and pulled into the parking lot before dialing the number again. She asked the receptionist to tell Geoff that she had his cell phone and he needed to run down and get it from her.

By the time Geoff met her outside, Dara was standing beside the car with tears streaming down her face.

"What happened? Is Timmy okay?" Geoff yelled as he ran toward her.

"Yes! Timmy is fine!" Dara stammered. "It's *this*!" she said with obvious anger as she handed Geoff his phone. The provocative photo was on the screen.

"Your online girlfriend has been texting all morning."

Geoff's face turned scarlet as he took the phone out of her hand.

He tried to deny that he knew this woman. He fumbled and stammered his outrage that someone would send such messages and a photo to him.

"I don't believe you!" Dara shouted between sobs. "How could you? I have to go. I left Timmy with a neighbor and need to go get him."

Geoff tried to reach for her, but she hopped into the car and sped away before he could offer up any more lies.

Later that night Geoff came clean, or so Dara thought. His story sounded real, convincing, and pretty remorseful. He said he'd been curious and started experimenting online.

"It's incredible what's available on some of these sites," he said in an innocent-sounding tone.

"I never meant to actually contact anyone. It just got out of control. This woman emailed me, and the next thing I knew, we were texting each other. I'm so sorry. It will never happen again."

Dara wanted so desperately to believe him. One mistake was just that—one mistake. She accepted his apology, but doubt needled her. Her world was scrambled, and she didn't know what to do. She wanted to trust Geoff, but a nagging feeling told her she couldn't.

The next day Dara checked Geoff's whereabouts every hour and looked through every business card he'd emptied from his coat after his last business trip. One of the restaurants' business cards was wholly unfamiliar to her. Her heart raced as she began to panic.

That night Dara and Geoff had a big argument about his behavior and her doubts. Then he clammed up and slept downstairs. She couldn't stand it. She loved him and hated him all at the same time.

Living in Aftershock

You may be able to identify with Dara's story. For most women who face a devastating experience like this, the details might not be exactly the same, but the results often are.

There are many women whose husbands lead secret lives of pornography use or other sexual compulsions. This appalling discovery sends a massive shock wave through a woman's life. Like a tsunami smashing into a peaceful shoreline, the unforeseen revelation of a husband's lies and sexual behavior ravages everything in its path and sweeps away any remaining illusions of a secure and happy marriage.

Unfortunately, like natural disasters, relational disasters often get worse before they get better. A tsunami isn't a single wave; it's more like a wave train. According to scientists, the aftershocks following an initial cataclysm can be equally dangerous. They're vast, unpredictable, and capable of collapsing damaged buildings that survived the original shock.

In the same way, some husbands wait weeks or months after the initial shocking revelation before admitting to other sordid behavior. After years of shameful self-talk, many men cope by minimizing and suppressing their sexual history, even deceiving themselves. As a result, they don't initially understand or remember all of the things they need to confess. Or in spite of their best cover-up efforts, new evidence comes to light and exposes them.

Some men who commit to a recovery process make a full confession quickly and clearly, but for most men, it takes weeks to grapple with reality and gain the skills to fully disclose their secrets. But staggered disclosures are usually more hurtful to wives than getting the whole truth up front.

Staggered Disclosures

It's important to understand the phenomenon of staggered disclosures because your husband may divulge more details about his behavior over time. This is also why it's useful to get professional help early on, though couples rarely do. The vast majority stumble through the early weeks of their crisis as the wife tries to extract all the details of her husband's bad behaviors, and the husband struggles with how to reveal more to his wife. Such interactions are so emotionally charged and complex that objective guidance from a well-trained professional is virtually essential to wade through the muck. If you are still new in your process, do all you can to get help at the earliest stage of disclosure.

My heart goes out to the many faithful wives who struggle to save their marriages but get knocked down again and again as the aftershocks keep coming. Being aware that there may be more to your husband's story can help lessen the shock if additional betrayals are revealed.

Knowing about staggered disclosures may motivate you and your husband to seek help sooner rather than trying to unravel the tangled web of your complicated relationship on your own.

The following examples of staggered disclosures may seem surprising or extreme to you. Yet they're situations described by women who suffered through their husbands' staggered disclosures. (The husbands' names have been changed.)

- "My husband, Connor, emphatically claimed he only viewed pornography and nothing more. But following a routine gynecology exam, the doctor said I had an STD [sexually transmitted disease]."
- "My husband was still on probation for viewing pornography on his workplace computer when his employer found new evidence. He was immediately fired, and we lost everything we saved for."
- "I was offended when Cooper confessed to going to strip bars, but he assured me that he had stopped years earlier. He was supposed to be on a business trip, but then he had a heart attack at the home of his secretary just twenty miles away."
- "Ever since we got married seventeen years ago, my husband and I have argued because he flirts with every female in sight, even though he denies it. Our senior pastor knocked on the door last night to report that a woman in the congregation had accused my husband of fondling her."
- "When my husband was in seminary, I was proud of him for getting help for his pornography addiction; he said he was cured. We are pastoring our third church, and his assistant found pornography on the church computer. She told the elders, and now everybody in church knows."

- "I never, ever got over the humiliation of Brayden's affair during our honeymoon in Hawaii. I got a call Saturday that he was seriously injured, so I rushed to the emergency room. His girlfriend was crying by his bedside."
- "I agreed to watch porn with my husband the first year we were married, but Jeb finally agreed with me that it was wrong. On our fifth anniversary, he announced with a smile that he'd bought a membership for a couples' swinger club—like I should be happy."
- "I was sick to my stomach when I found my husband's regular [heterosexual] pornography. But then I found his homosexual porn. He later said that he didn't think it was necessary to talk about his childhood sexual play with other little boys; he considered it in his past."
- "Miles got abusive whenever I asked him to stop watching adult movies on TV. But I got a call from the police this weekend; he was arrested for being a Peeping Tom."

Take Hold of Your Imagination

These examples of staggered disclosure aren't intended to throw your emotions into a tailspin or cause your imagination to run rampant. You need to be well informed, but don't grab on to every example as something that will happen to you.

Your husband's response might be completely different from the stories these women shared. You may be blessed with a husband who chose to tell you immediately when he realized how out-of-control his behaviors were. Or perhaps as soon as his sexual compulsions were exposed, he told you the entire truth, with no secrets withheld. Some husbands are truly repentant and remorseful with a godly sorrow, eager to mend their ways, and ready to cooperate and seek treatment.

If that describes the man in your life, your road to recovery won't be nearly so rough. So don't leap to extreme conclusions about your husband's sexual compulsions, but also understand that you're living in the aftershock of one crashing wave of destruction.

Chapter 7 will provide specific guidelines to follow, whether your husband is motivated to work toward inner transformation or is resistant to change. But right now, while your emotions are raging or numb, just hang on. Even if you fear there is no hope for your marriage, take a deep breath. Try to believe that you've taken a valuable step forward by opening this book.

You Are Not Alone!

If you're feeling isolated, I want to assure you that you aren't reading the words of a woman who has lived an unscathed, victorious life floating above the clouds. I walked through my own valley of pain a number of years ago. I've been wounded by my own bad choices and the offensive behavior of others in my life. In addition to my professional credentials, I come to you with the experiences of my own hurtful past.

I've also worked with hundreds of couples over the past two decades who were in circumstances similar to yours. I understand what you're going through, and I want to help by coming alongside you as a sister and a fellow sharer in your difficult journey. The Bible tells us that God comforts and encourages us in every trouble so that we will be able to comfort and encourage others with the comfort we've received from Him (2 Corinthians 1:3-4). I now know that working through my heartaches leads to peace, joy, and healing. My earnest prayer is that you will also benefit from facing and working through your pain so that you can experience God's wonderful healing.

A Large Sisterhood

Here's another story about a cell phone:

> Hannah hadn't told anyone, not a single person, about her troubled marriage. On the contrary, for fifteen years she'd been wearing a smile and telling everybody that she and her husband, Noah, had a great relationship. If only folks could have taken a look behind closed doors or seen the pain and questions in her heart!
>
> In reality, Hannah and Noah's marriage was filled with a multitude of problems. When she vocalized her frustration, he invariably shut down and withdrew. Neither of them knew how to resolve conflict in a healthy way, so no argument ended well. Their ongoing resentment spilled into the bedroom, resulting in an entirely unsatisfactory sex life, especially for her. But Hannah told herself that this was due to their crazy schedule and the fatigue that comes from raising three active children—factors that did make it difficult for them to find time for one another. Still, she couldn't shake a nagging feeling that something was wrong at a much deeper level.
>
> Then it happened. Hannah's suspicions led her to pick up Noah's cell phone while he was in the shower. She quickly scrolled through his text messages and

discovered he had been texting suggestive messages and images to an old high-school girlfriend. In one fell swoop, all of her worst fears seemed to be confirmed. Suddenly that nagging feeling made sense. Apparently there was something more to their lack of intimacy than mere busyness and fatigue.

Hannah was waiting for Noah when he came out of the bathroom, wrapped in a towel and scrambling around looking for his phone.

"Have you seen my phone?" he asked. "I need to make a quick call."

When she confronted Noah with the disturbing intimate messages she'd found, he scolded her, accused her of snooping, and dismissed her like a naughty child. He was just a normal male having a little fun that had started with high-school companions on social media, he argued.

"What's the big deal about chatting with an old friend? Besides," he told Hannah, "I will never meet up with her in person. Don't make a federal case out of this. It's not like adultery, so just drop it."

Wounded and confused, Hannah added to her own pain by putting herself down and feeling guilty for being suspicious in the first place. Life slipped back into its normal frantic routine, but as the days passed, it became obvious that she and Noah were drifting further and further apart. He approached her less and less often for any kind of intimacy. And when she took the initiative, he simply brushed her off.

After numerous attempts to get Noah to change,

Hannah finally took the risk of sharing her secret with someone else. That someone was me.

A Troubling Reality

When I was pregnant with my firstborn, and later as I raised her, the women I knew shared their parenting knowledge—helpful information they had gathered by trial and error. Moms coached other moms, and we all learned from one another.

Sexual compulsions, on the other hand, aren't usually a topic women discuss when they get together, and stories like Hannah's are all too prevalent. She finally did talk to me in a professional setting, but she told none of her friends or family. Shock and pain reverberated inside her as she longed for answers on how to cope with the aftershock of her husband's behavior. Hannah was unprepared for the kind of shock that washed over her.

I never thought this would happen to me, you might be saying to yourself.

You've probably been aware of the widespread use of pornography but never really thought about having to deal with such a hurtful issue in your own life.

The sad truth is that pornography use and other compulsive sexual behaviors are extremely common in contemporary society. The problem is extensive, both inside and outside the church. The reasons for this are obvious: declining morals, universal internet access, sexual objectification of other human beings, salacious imagery on TV and smartphones, and increasing cultural pressure to tolerate deviant behavior.

Compulsive sexual behaviors may be common, but that doesn't make them any less painful and destructive. All anyone has to do is google the words *pornography addiction* to find countless statistics about its use and equal quantities of advice on what to do if you're a victim of its damaging effects.

Please do not google any aspects of this topic! Information found online and in some books gives terribly conflicting advice to the undiscerning reader, such as "Learn to be a better lover, don't tell anyone, watch pornography with him, and join a couples' swingers club" to the opposite advice: "Kick him out of the house, expose him in front of the family, or find the best lawyer you can afford."

Who can answer your haunting questions or provide appropriate coaching? Unfortunately, good and healthy input is hard to come by. If you somehow find the courage to ask your friends, you may receive encouraging words of comfort but not really any helpful advice.

A friend may have sufficient suggestions for potty training, but when your marriage, family, and entire future are at stake, you want to be sure to get appropriate professional advice, along with any comfort or well-meaning encouragement your friends can offer. You need well-researched information to fill in the gaps. You need comfort, hope, realism, and some practical direction. Hopefully that is how this book will help.

A Critical Turning Point

Nearly every couple I've worked with through the years whose marriage survived looks back and credits the wife's response and her choices for redemptive hope as the critical turning point for the damaged relationship.

The wives in these situations committed to heal and grow personally in the hopes that their husbands would do the same. They faced a choice: They could close the door to a continued relationship or leave it open just enough for their husbands to step through it toward healing.

You may struggle with the thought of even wanting a restored relationship with your husband. Your trust may be so shattered that you're at the point of despair. Right now, you might harbor so much disappointment that you've literally slammed doors shut to gain distance from your husband. I understand. I really do.

Giving a second chance to someone who might not deserve it is often beyond our human ability. But extending hope, grace, and an honorable "fight" for your marriage is more than a feeling; it's a God thing. It's strength that comes from beyond you, strength that you can willfully access as part of Christ's ongoing work in your life.

You will need support from others as you decide to fight for your marriage. Surround yourself with *wise* advice. Some people would have you roll over in passivity, while others might justifiably be so angry for you that they'd pay your lawyer bill today!

The decision to invest in giving your marriage a chance isn't a guarantee of success, but it's *right*, and it reflects God's heart and hope. He always aims to repair broken things and make them even *better* than they were before.

The following promises that God gave to the Israelites can be encouraging truths for you as well:

> Behold, I am doing a new thing;
>   now it springs forth, do you not perceive it?
> I will make a way in the wilderness
>   and rivers in the desert.
>
> ISAIAH 43:19

> Instead of your shame there shall be a double portion;
> > instead of dishonor they shall rejoice in their lot;
> therefore in their land they shall possess a double portion;
> > they shall have everlasting joy.
>
> ISAIAH 61:7

The Spiritual Light of Christ

Satan wants to kill your marriage. While plenty has already been done to threaten it, don't succumb further to his death lies and schemes. Don't cope by going into denial about the painful truth of what's been occurring, but *do* strain to see the light of Christ rising on you in the midst of the storm.

Your world might seem quite dark to you now. I imagine you've had nights when, like me, you cried until you didn't think you could cry anymore. But then you did! King David could empathize with us. He wrote, "I am weary with my moaning; every night I flood my bed with tears; I drench my couch with my weeping" (Psalm 6:6).

The popular phrase "The darkest hour is just before dawn" is true! But we can be encouraged to know that even though "weeping may tarry for the night . . . joy comes with the morning" (Psalm 30:5).

Your trial is time limited. The dawn *is* coming. Joy is on the horizon. I can make that claim with full confidence because I have witnessed desperate and broken people being restored. For dozens of years, I have counseled women married to men with out-of-control sexual compulsions. When I first meet these women, they often fear there is no hope for them or their marriages. They are living in a darkness that clouds their vision and prevents them from seeing the light ahead.

But they make a commitment to move forward, step by step, regardless of their situations. They learn about healthy boundaries and self-care, which give them better footing and a sustainable self-respecting pace through this trial. You can make that commitment too. I encourage you to read on and keep going, even when times are difficult and you want to give up.

Difficulties *will* come. The burden you presently carry along with the normal busyness of life may wear you out physically, emotionally, and spiritually. You might wonder how you can possibly find time to keep reading and doing the necessary work for healing to occur.

I'm praying that you will hit the Pause button, take a deep breath, and choose *not* to act on those negative thoughts and raw nerves.

I hope you'll take advantage of the tools in the following chapters. You'll be learning about yourself, the betrayal process, and how your husband likely developed his destructive behaviors. You'll also learn about the dynamics of your marital relationship—the good and the bad—and how you got to the place you are today.

And you'll have the opportunity to make choices that have proved effective in restoring and transforming shattered marriages while still taking care of your own heart as well.

Don't give up!

REFLECTION

Call upon me in the day of trouble;
> I will deliver you, and you shall glorify me.

PSALM 50:15

> The floods have lifted up, O Lord,
>   the floods have lifted up their voice;
>   the floods lift up their roaring.
> Mightier than the thunders of many waters,
>   mightier than the waves of the sea,
>   the Lord on high is mighty!
>
> PSALM 93:3-4

QUESTIONS

1. Do you have a special journal for recording your thoughts and prayers as you move through this journey? You'll need one. If you don't have one yet, ask yourself, *What's keeping me from getting a journal and taking a step to write, express, and sort out my feelings on paper? How can I remedy that and invest in what's recommended?*

2. What do the verses from Psalms 50 and 93 say to you today? When or in what circumstances each day do you most need to remember these truths? Post these verses where you're most likely to be at those moments of your day.

3. Psalm 50:15 reminds us that we can honor God even when we're going through something *deeply* troubling. What does honoring God and feeling the fulfillment of obedience and integrity look like for you in this moment?

PRAYER

Lord, the "floods" of my problems and my husband's problems have lifted up, and I feel waves of aftershock pounding against me. I'm calling on You, trusting You. And I will honor You. Enable me to do this every day as I'm reading this book, seeking Your deliverance through the comfort of Your Word, and relying on Your help to take the practical steps I'm just beginning to learn about. In Jesus' name, amen.

CHAPTER 2

"CAN I TRUST MY EMOTIONS?"

*Weeping may tarry for the night,
but joy comes with the morning.*

PSALM 30:5

SOPHIA WAS A CONFIDENT PUBLIC SPEAKER and respected community leader, but you wouldn't have known it to look at her. When she first came to my office, she sat speechless and motionless, with tears streaming down her cheeks. Eventually she choked out the words, "I feel ashamed and humiliated. I feel like such a fool. Everyone else probably knew about Mason's affairs long ago, and I'm his wife. Does he think I'm so stupid that he can commit adultery and I'll never figure it out? Now I'm ready to pay him back, and I'll do it! He'll be sorry once I get done ruining him."

Another wife, Alli, found out six months ago that her husband had been using pornography several nights a week after she had fallen asleep. They had been married three years and had no children, which gave them the time and energy to enjoy an active sex life. After weeks of her husband's excuses for not having sex as often as they had in the past, she became suspicious. One night Alli went to his office and found him viewing pornography on his computer. He was so "engaged" with the photo on his screen that she walked all the way up to him and saw the image herself. Since then, Alli has been stuck in a swamp of anger, grief, fear, and myriad other feelings she's unable to even name.

How Do *You* Feel?

Alli was overwhelmed by the emotions that paralyzed her and held her captive. Sophia was ready to strike back. Do you feel like either of these women? Or are you experiencing a completely different reaction to the pain you feel?

When the tsunami and aftershocks of your husband's sexual exploits have slammed into you, it's not unusual to feel as if you're spiraling out of control. Or you may feel determined to pull yourself out of this mess like Wonder Woman.

Whatever you're feeling, it's important to realize that your emotions matter. They are powerful and unpredictable—and they're normal. They also need your attention. Your feelings may shift without warning from one extreme to another. A barrage of bitter words can spew out of your mouth at the most inappropriate moments. In the next instant, you may feel completely cold and numb. It's like riding a roller coaster that you can't get off!

Emotions Are Neither Right nor Wrong

Unfortunately, many of us have been taught some damaging and false principles about emotions. You might have been told that it's wrong to feel angry, that you shouldn't feel sad, or that your faith is weak if you're emotional.

But your emotions are neither right nor wrong. In fact, they can be your best friends if you pay attention to the messages they're attempting to convey. Think of emotions as flashing lights on the dashboard of your car that let you know something is wrong. If you understand what a light means, you know what the problem is and can attend to it so that your car will once again operate the way it was built to operate.

The same is true for you. A light is flashing on the dashboard of your mind. Powerful emotions battle for your attention. You might feel anger and sadness at the same time, or anxiety may have you in its grip. You weren't created to live with this pain and confusion. The flashing light is telling you to attend to what is going on inside you.

Responding to the Flashing Light

Right now you may feel no ability to respond to your erratic emotions with any control at all. Of course you can't! You can't be expected to respond well to the terrible news you've just received. But help is on the way!

Stop for a moment and take a few deep breaths. Remember, you are not alone. You *will* get through this. You may not feel that way now, but please believe me.

It's not uncommon for women to take action based on their emotions, which often results in making poor decisions. You might feel compelled to *do* something, or you might want to just shut yourself away in your room. But please don't do anything drastic or make any important long-term decisions right now. And while you may need to spend some time alone, don't isolate yourself from family and friends.

Think about that flashing light on the dashboard of your

car. How you respond to the light is very important. Anger or frustration could cause you to lose focus on the surrounding traffic. Fear of the car blowing up could cause your blood pressure to skyrocket. Obsession with getting to an appointment on time could lead you to ignore the problem, causing even more damage. How you respond determines what happens to your car and, more importantly, to yourself as the driver.

How you respond to the aftershock you're experiencing now will determine how well you'll manage your life in the days and weeks ahead.

Avoid Two Common Mistakes

Let's consider Sophia's and Alli's stories again. Sophia was ready to ruin her husband after finding out about his affair. In talking with her further, I found out that her parents went through a nasty divorce when Sophia was around twelve years old. The arguments were seared into Sophia's memory:

> I remember hearing [my parents] yell during any fight they ever had. My dad would get really mad if dinner wasn't ready when he walked in the door after work, and then my mom would yell back even louder. When arguments grew more frequent over bigger issues, like whether to move to a larger house or not, the fighting got more intense. There would be yelling and storming out of the house and leaving nasty notes on the refrigerator. Sometimes my dad would just disappear for a few days.
>
> I hated it! But I just thought that was the way

"CAN I TRUST MY EMOTIONS?"

all married people acted when they were mad about anything, from a late dinner to selling a house.

Alli had the opposite reaction to her husband's affair and their eventual divorce. She actually didn't come into my office and begin to fully deal with his infidelity until more than a decade after it happened.

After my husband ran off with his girlfriend, I just shut down emotionally. I moved back in with my parents and acted like I was fine. My mom and dad never asked me about what really happened, and I never offered any information.

Growing up, we didn't talk about feelings. My two sisters and I answered when spoken to and stayed quiet otherwise. Even my parents verbalized very little. Avoiding conflict seemed to be the norm. I only remember a few times I would see my mother shut herself in her bedroom and come out later with red eyes and a sadness that was silently evident. Only one time did I ask her what was wrong. She quickly said, "Nothing!"

Like Sophia and Alli, all of us are deeply influenced by the environments we grew up in. Most child development experts agree that the first five to six years of life bear the greatest influence on personality formation. Our primary caregivers modeled *their* ways of expressing emotions, which we unknowingly absorbed or now react to. The problem arises when a family's pattern of either overreacting or underreacting interferes with an individual's ability to cope well with life stressors.

If you tend to overreact, venting your feelings without regard for the time or place or the choice of your words, you'll probably disrupt any meaningful communication or movement toward potential restoration.

If you typically underreact by burying your feelings or denying them, your response will be nonproductive. Imagine holding a beach ball underwater. That's what it's like when you attempt to conceal the pain you've endured as a result of your husband's behavior. Burying your feelings requires a lot of attention and drains your energy. As the days go by, you'll find yourself trying to hold two beach balls underwater at the same time, or even three or four if enough months or years go by. You'll quickly discover you're facing an impossible task.

What a relief it is to stop fighting the inevitable and simply let the truth and the accompanying feelings rise to the surface to be addressed in the appropriate way they deserve!

If you want to avoid the extremes of either burying your emotions or acting them out fully, it's important to make an effort to understand yourself at a deeper level. That's a loaded statement! Understanding yourself at a deeper level takes time and self-care. The tools at the end of each chapter will help you work through this process.

If you haven't started journaling your thoughts and feelings, I strongly encourage you to do so. What you write in your journal is for your eyes only. Don't worry about what you express or how you express it. God can use this exercise to help you dig down to the parts of your soul where the pain is the greatest.

As you read through this book, journal your feelings, and

work through the activities at the end of each chapter, you'll turn that statement into a reality. You'll not only understand yourself and your emotions at a deeper level, but you'll also gain greater insight about who you are. As a result—and with guidance from God's Spirit and hopefully a trusted counselor—you'll be able to think more clearly and respond wisely to your situation.

Maybe you grew up in a home where emotions were openly and effectively expressed. If you did, you were blessed with good role models, but you still need to watch out so you don't slip into overreacting or underreacting. It's easy to do when your emotions are raging. You have sustained a devastating shock and need to understand yourself and your feelings at a more profound level.

Identifying and Understanding Your Emotions

There are five basic emotions: mad, bad, sad, glad, and afraid. Since it's safe to assume that "glad" isn't one of the emotions you're experiencing right now, we'll look at the remaining four emotions.

Mad/Angry

It's only natural that you'll feel *mad* or intensely *angry* with your husband; he has betrayed you and destroyed your trust. There is nothing wrong with admitting this and taking ownership of your reaction to his behavior. The Bible acknowledges that anger is a normal emotion, but it also warns us not to give it a foothold in our lives: "Be angry and do not sin; do not let the sun go down on your anger, and give no opportunity to the devil" (Ephesians 4:26-27).

You may be thinking, *What? How can anger be okay if it also* gives *"opportunity to the devil"*? Although I can understand your reaction, it's important to recognize that there are two types of angry responses:

1. *Healthy, protective, and righteous anger.* This is the kind of anger we need in the face of sin or injustice—for example, the anger Jesus experienced when He threw the corrupt money changers out of the Temple.
2. *Destructive anger.* This type of anger is involved when people respond inappropriately or in sinful ways, multiplying the damage as they retaliate and exact revenge.

Let's look at an example of destructive anger:

Cindy was furious when she found out about her husband's use of pornography, which had led to an affair. They quickly separated and were presumably headed for divorce. Every day Cindy was consumed with thoughts of hurting her husband as much as he had hurt her. Their two young children remained with Cindy during the week and stayed with their father on the weekend. Cindy's anger burned and festered with each phone call to her attorney. She raised her voice no matter who was around, including her children. After these calls, she would immediately call a friend and repeat every detail that upset her. Her anger blocked out any concern for what her children were hearing. Within a few months, Cindy was diagnosed with hypertension, and both of her children were showing signs of stress in school.

Like Cindy, you may be completely justified in feeling righteous anger. But if ungodly reactions have a grip on you, you're in danger. Think about it for a moment: How harmful and destructive are your angry reactions? Are you feeding your anger in a way that is caustic and corrosive and merely harbors your wrath? This volatile state of mind is fertile ground for two of the most damaging by-products of your pain to grow: revenge and bitterness.

Seeking revenge can feel really good—for a little while. You may be so wounded that you begin to think in terms of ruining your husband's reputation, career, and friendships. You may even be tempted to pull your children into the conflict and turn them against their father. Or maybe you've entertained having an affair yourself.

Be careful!

Women who act out these vengeful thoughts inevitably regret it. By the time they come to see me, they're usually grappling with deep remorse or the agonizing consequences of what they did. Their actions have only intensified their pain and created more chaos. Their anger has reigned supreme day and night, and they're obsessed with thoughts of revenge. The devil has indeed taken the opportunity to profit from their anger.

Maybe you aren't seeking revenge, but you find yourself living with deep internalized bitterness. The Bible speaks clearly on this issue: "See to it that no one fails to obtain the grace of

God; that no 'root of bitterness' springs up and causes trouble, and by it many become defiled" (Hebrews 12:15).

If a "root of bitterness" remains inside you, your soul will be damaged. You will miss the grace of God you so desperately need. God wants to comfort you, heal you, and restore you. He wants to protect you from the inevitable harm that bitterness can inflict on your physical body as well as your soul. Go to Him for help.

At the end of this day, be totally honest with God. Tell Him *exactly* how you feel. He loves you unconditionally and will never abandon you. So be as transparent as possible. Ask the Lord to help you release any vengeful thoughts or bitterness and show you how to respond to your anger in a healthy way. As you read further, I'll offer suggestions for moving through your anger in beneficial ways that lead to healing and constructive action.

Bad/Ashamed

Feeling bad can sometimes be anger turned inward. You may blame yourself for not suspecting your husband's pornography use or compulsive sexual behaviors sooner. Sophia, the betrayed wife whose story appears at the beginning of this chapter, felt this way.

"Am I just stupid or what?" she asked the first time we sat down together.

I've heard *many* similar self-condemning statements from women who feel ashamed and berate themselves for being so clueless.

If you're one of those women, I want to help you realize that a person doesn't have to be stupid to be deceived. People who engage in deception and who fear being exposed are clever and skilled in covering up their adulterous actions. After years of lying, they become such masters of deception that it's often difficult to discern.

When a typically honest person tells a lie, the conscience produces an internal tension that usually shows up on the outside. That's why it's generally easy to catch children in their lies. They haven't lived long enough to become skilled in the art of masking their actions. It's different with practiced, habitual liars. Such people deceive themselves *before* they set out to deceive others. They actually believe their own lies, which explains why they're so good at deceiving others.

They may also be masters of manipulation, convincing the keenest discerner that their lies are true. A woman can be competent at seeing through a ruse most of the time and *still* overlook the signs of her husband's infidelity. After all, this is the man you pledged your loyalty to and allowed access to the most intimate aspects of your mind, body, and spirit.

Finally, if you continue to feel truly bad and ashamed of yourself, you might be carrying *transferred guilt*. A transfer of guilt happens when the guilty party lays his guilt on the innocent party. For example, your husband has committed an act of betrayal against you and your marriage, but he convinces you, or you convince yourself, that *you're* the one to blame for that act. The lie is that you are guilty of these unfaithful actions. The result is that you feel ashamed even though you aren't the one to blame.

If you're carrying transferred guilt, work on changing your thinking from the damaging lie to the freeing truth: *Your husband is responsible for his own actions.* While you always want to examine your own life and heart with integrity and humility, don't take his guilt upon yourself. It's not yours!

Sad/Grieving

Sadness is part of the grieving process, but it's not the whole picture. You might feel sad about any number of things:

- Your daughter left for college.
- Your friend is moving away.
- The vet says your dog needs major surgery.

I don't mean to trivialize any of these sad occasions, but I do want to put them into perspective. Events of this kind might make you feel sad, but it would be misleading to compare sadness with the overwhelming emotional weight of grief from betrayal or marital infidelity. Consider Nancy's story, when she was forced to grieve the loss of her childhood dream of a perfect husband:

> "I want a Cinderella dress," six-year-old Nancy told her mother as they walked out of the movie theater. They had just watched the iconic film *Cinderella* that has inspired millions of little girls since its first release in 1950.
>
> Nancy got the dress she wanted. And eventually she got her Prince Charming—or so she thought. But her dreams were crushed when her husband began using pornography and stopped having intimate relations with her a few years after their marriage.

Countless women like Nancy hold on to the powerful childhood dream of Prince Charming sweeping into their lives and carrying them away to live happily ever after. Why wouldn't they? The story of Cinderella is a beautiful, emotionally charged image of being deeply loved and faithfully cared for, with promises of joy, acceptance, and all things good.

Unfortunately, it doesn't reflect the reality of being married to a fallible human being. No marriage is perfect, no matter how beautiful or wonderful it is. When the lie wrapped up in this fairy tale is revealed, grief descends, and sadness dives to an unimaginable depth. But grief can be a doorway to the truth: While your spouse might be a desirable and good mate, he isn't a good savior. Grieving the loss of this popular fantasy and clinging more fully to Christ is key to the potential resurrection of your marriage.

In his book *A Grief Observed*, C. S. Lewis described the grief he experienced after the death of his wife:

> Part of every misery is, so to speak . . . the fact that you don't merely suffer but have to keep on thinking about the fact that you suffer. I not only live each endless day in grief, but live each day thinking about living each day in grief.[1]

Clearly, grief is much more than merely sadness.

Although you might not be dealing with the physical death of a spouse, you are dealing with the daily reality of grief that Lewis described—especially in these early days of aftershock.

I've lost track of the numbers of brokenhearted wives who have told me, "We had a marriage made in heaven, until I found his pornography," or "My husband is perfect in every way, except he keeps having affairs."

It's understandable you feel this way if you were influenced by the dreamy image of a romantic Prince Charming, but you might not be aware of the unrealistic view you had of the flawed man you married. Perhaps you kept him teetering on a pedestal for a while, but now he has fallen off.

I'm not defending your husband's behavior, but it's important to realize that your original perceptions of him might have been based, in part, on your longings and the high ideals you had for your life, rather than the full variety of both good and bad qualities he displayed. A significant part of such idealism has to do with your deep desires. On your wedding day, you were the princess, the adored and beloved object of your groom's affection. You thought it would last forever, but you don't feel that way now. You feel sad, depressed, and far from regal.

The good news is that things don't have to stay this way. You are even more regal than you may have imagined. You are the daughter of the King. God loves you unconditionally. His Son took all shame and human guilt upon Himself, and as a result, God offers redemption in your circumstances. You don't live in a fairy tale but in the truth that God is in the business of healing and restoring lives. Psalm 107:6 says, "Then they [the redeemed] cried to the LORD in their trouble, and he delivered them from their distress."

As you grieve the loss of your dream, you can choose to receive peace and hope from God. And I pray that your husband finds it too. Oddly enough, grief can be instructive and lead to hope!

A word of caution: If you don't choose to authentically seek God in the midst of this crisis, you could be in danger of either burying your grief or getting stuck in a condition called *complicated grief.* Alli, whose story you read at the beginning of this chapter, experienced this.

In complicated grief, painful emotions are so long-lasting that you have trouble accepting the loss and resuming normal activities and responsibilities. Often, this happens because the trauma of the present moment has opened *old* wounds. In part, you're responding all over again to the calamities and disappointments of the past. Like a tsunami that stirs up underwater debris buried decades earlier, your current hurts stir up all of your painful memories from the past and bring them to the surface.

Alli is an extreme example, but her story illustrates the point that time alone doesn't heal all pain. By the time Alli came to see me, almost two decades had passed since her crisis. Her painful emotions had held her captive all that time. She complicated her grieving process by living with that pain for so long.

Naturally, if your husband continues misbehaving sexually, telling lies, and expressing sorrow or remorse, but then repeats the same pattern again and again, you'll have greater difficulty moving forward. You may be in that situation now and feel truly stuck. But you don't need to *stay* stuck. You can learn how to get out of that rut and alter your responses in a way that tests your husband's resolve to heal and frees you from the merry-go-round.

Please heed this important advice: Complicated grief can slide into deep depression and then into suicidal thinking. If this describes you in any manner, please tell a trusted friend, a family member, or a pastor and schedule an appointment as soon as possible with a therapist for a professional assessment, or go directly to the local emergency room.

Afraid/Fearful/Anxious

Fear is closely tied to grief. Grieving is about past events and what has *already* happened. Fear is about the future and what *might* happen. C. S. Lewis acknowledged this relationship in the opening sentence of *A Grief Observed*: "No one ever told me that grief felt so like fear."[2]

When your marriage is in trouble, it's not uncommon to quickly escalate your current situation into a worst-case scenario and become afraid and anxious. What-ifs can plague you:

- *What if my husband chooses his secret life over me and refuses to stop using pornography?*
- *What if he doesn't love me anymore?*
- *What if he loves someone else and abandons me and our children?*

The list of possible bad outcomes is endless.

Fearing the fulfillment of the what-ifs is like having a stomachache and thinking it's cancer. It could be. But it could also be a multitude of far less serious things. Most of us know when we have a physical symptom that it isn't particularly helpful to go online and read the worst-case scenario for that symptom—especially if we have active imaginations.

Fixating on the what-ifs is of no benefit whatsoever. As the famous preacher Charles Spurgeon observed, "It has been well said that our anxiety does not empty to-morrow of its sorrows, but only empties to-day of its strength."[3]

You can counteract your fear by focusing on your recovery. One way to accomplish that task is to realize that God cares for

"CAN I TRUST MY EMOTIONS?"

you more than you can humanly imagine. You can be assured that He wants to help you conquer fear because He gave us 365 Scripture verses that say, "Fear not," "Fret not," and "Do not be anxious." God wouldn't tell you *not* to fear if you wouldn't benefit from seeking to obey His command. He knows that you *can* replace fear with a hopeful attitude that originates with Him.

On our own, it's a challenge to reverse the physical, mental, and spiritual impact of anxiety. But God gives us a helpful prescription to keep anxiety at bay:

> Do not be anxious about anything, but in everything by prayer and supplication with thanksgiving let your requests be made known to God. And the peace of God, which surpasses all understanding, will guard your hearts and your minds in Christ Jesus.
>
> PHILIPPIANS 4:6-7

Leave your very natural anxiety in God's care. This is a *spiritual* exercise. You can't put your worries in a physical box and stick it in some corner for God to come and pick up. But you *can* mentally gather your anxious feelings and place them in God's care. So let go! Repeatedly set down your fears and grab hold of the hopeful promises God is offering you. Your practical journaling exercises and the listening ears of your most trusted support-team members are key outlets that can help you identify, evaluate, and release your specific fears and anxieties. Pretending you don't have anxieties isn't helpful, but bringing them before God and others will increase your comfort and calm your anxious, fearful heart.

Specific Action Steps

There are specific action steps you can take to deal with your emotions in a healthy way. The goal is to learn to become aware of your emotions, interpret their meaning, and use them to communicate productively, decisively, and even respectfully in your situation. During desperate times, it can be difficult to sort out your feelings and make sense of them because as human beings, we're capable of experiencing a wide range of emotions. But emotions can provide you with valuable information if you develop an awareness of them and embrace them.

To become more aware of your emotions, you need to be able to distinguish primary emotions from secondary emotions. *Primary emotions* are feelings we experience in *direct* response to an event and/or a specific stimulus. They're initial reactions or responses we have that are natural, instinctive, or unthinking. A *secondary emotion* is "an emotion about an emotion." For example, you might feel guilty or ashamed about the fact that you feel sad or lonely. Secondary emotions are often learned responses to life or what we think the "script" *should* be.

Now that you know how to recognize primary and secondary emotions, let's look at some helpful steps you can take to deal with your emotions in a healthy way.

1. *Identify the primary emotions you're experiencing.* Again, primary emotions are the "first natural responses" to something that happens. Sometimes your body will offer clues as to what you're feeling. Tightness in the chest, a snarled nose, heaviness or strain around the eyes. Take body cues and give these visceral reactions the most fitting emotional label. The awareness of the initial reaction

"CAN I TRUST MY EMOTIONS?"

is helpful so that you can decide what to do in response to it over time. It helps you honor what you're experiencing and then make decisions as to how to care for or direct that reaction. So pause for a moment. Think about what you're feeling as you react or respond to an event, and if possible, jot down a word or two describing the emotion and what triggered it. Later on, journal in more detail about the feelings you identified.

2. *Dig deeper to gain access to buried (secondary) emotions.* Why is digging deeper necessary? Because, as I mentioned earlier, the environments in which we grew up and the people who raised us had a profound influence on our development, and as a result, we quickly revert to the relational style and emotional responses we learned from our upbringings. Digging into buried secondary emotions can help you evaluate the thinking that drives them. Remember, secondary emotions are emotions about emotions, and you can often make conscious decisions that steer them to God's truth.

Here's an illustration of what I mean: A supervisor in a corporation called a departmental meeting and announced the company decision to begin keeping better production records. Each member of the group initially experienced apprehension, but if you look beneath the primary emotion to the secondary emotions, here's what you might discover:

- Person 1 felt *hopeful* and thought, *Good! Management will see there are problems and make needed improvements.*

- Person 2 felt *dread* and remarked, "Oh no! There will be layoffs." Depression quickly followed, and she withdrew for the rest of the day.

- Person 3 felt *excited*, thinking, *They'll see that I'm a valuable employee and give me a raise.*

- Person 4 felt *angry* with the establishment and made some nasty comments. That night, she took out her anger on her husband and children.

Interesting, isn't it? The entire group heard the same message, which initially resulted in the primary emotion of apprehension. That emotion triggered secondary emotions, which triggered a wide range of thoughts and actions. As this example illustrates, it's not what happens to us that matters but how we respond to it.

3. *Practice getting in touch with your emotions.* If this step is difficult for you, google "feelings wheel" or "emotions chart" to find words that describe how you feel. You might also initiate a game with your family at dinnertime and announce, "Whoever can name the most emotions they felt today wins." Or you could go online and search for cartoon faces of different emotions, which you can print for free and put on the refrigerator door.

4. *Increase your vocabulary for expressing various emotions.* The more specifically you identify your feelings, the more likely your spouse will understand. For example, the primary emotion "mad" might mean anything from

"annoyed" to "enraged," so it's important to use a word that accurately reflects what you feel.

5. *Practice communicating, "I feel _____ when you _____."* Countless clients report that using this suggestion alone decreased the length of their arguments and reduced the risk of an escalation. Remember, though, a feeling is expressed with *one word*, not a full sentence. In our culture, people who begin a sentence with "I feel" may assume they're expressing a feeling. A husband recently said, "I feel my wife is drifting away and having an affair." Instead of expressing a feeling, he was expressing a thought or opinion.

At this point you might be thinking, *Okay, I have a better understanding of my emotions now, but I still feel mad, bad, sad, or afraid.* If that's the case, don't get discouraged. Remember that you're in a spiritual struggle as well as a human one. It will take some time and practice to know how to best respond or work through each emotion, but in the midst of your pain, God will draw near as you draw near to Him and truly seek His peace. Whether or not you *feel* like doing so, keep following these steps and suggestions, and in time, you'll be well on your way toward honoring and responding to your range of emotions in a productive way!

REFLECTION
Spend a few minutes thinking about how deeply Jesus understands your feelings. He felt a flood of emotions too, yet He trusted His Father to stand beside Him and deliver Him from every trial.

QUESTIONS

1. When you were growing up, what emotions were expressed most often in your home?

2. What has been your strongest primary emotion recently: mad, bad, sad, or afraid? Think of a recent incident and identify your secondary emotions.

3. What emotions did you experience as you read this chapter?

4. Make a list of sentences that begin with "I feel _____ when you _____." Ask God which ones you should share with your husband.

5. At the end of each week or month, look back at the list of emotions you recorded daily in your journal. Note any changes or trends. This exercise will help you gain greater insight into yourself, and that's good!

PRAYER

Father, I want to share with You the reality that I'm often filled with conflicting emotions. I'm grateful I can bring every one of my feelings to You, and You will never reject or embarrass me for being honest. Thank You for hearing me and loving me. Help me identify my emotions so they don't spin out of control. Please hold my heart, Lord. It's breaking in two. Help me feel my emotions and respond to them wisely—the way You designed me to. In Jesus' name, amen.

CHAPTER 3

"WHAT WAS I THINKING?"

*Do not be conformed to this world, but be transformed
by the renewal of your mind, that by testing you
may discern what is the will of God, what is
good and acceptable and perfect.*

ROMANS 12:2

"I JUST CAN'T THINK STRAIGHT," Paula said as she sat in my office after discovering her husband's pornography use and online affair.

Paula was dressed to perfection. Her hairstyle, makeup, jewelry, and demeanor all reflected her corporate status as a senior executive and successfully hid the turmoil inside.

"I don't know how much longer I can keep it all together," she confided. "Our children are grown, so I don't have to work hard to fool them. But my job is so demanding that I really need to cope better than I am."

After we met several more times, Paula's primary challenge became evident: Her way of thinking about her situation was a major stumbling block. Although she wasn't aware of how her thoughts were keeping her trapped, they were definitely sabotaging her progress.

Distorted Thinking

Proverbs 23:7 (NKJV) says, "As [a man] thinks in his heart, so is he." Or to reflect Paula's story, we could say, "As Paula thinks in her heart, so is she."

Paula's thinking was understandable, but it wasn't in line with the truth. Initially she believed her husband's denial of his online behavior and denied her own doubts. When she finally admitted that he really was doing these things, she rationalized away any responsibility on his part, attributing his behavior to his high-pressure job. Soon her thoughts began to swing from optimism to pessimism. Then the negative thoughts took over, and she automatically dwelled on the worst-case scenario. When all else failed to help her cope, she resorted to overspiritualizing everything.

Paula was desperate for relief and arrived in my office with a tangle of distorted thinking. Maybe you can identify with her.

In the course of counseling, I've discovered that most wives, regardless of their education, socioeconomic status, or level of maturity, respond to their husbands' betrayals with predictable patterns of coping. I can identify with these women because of my own feeble attempts to cope.

I've been in similar places, and I know how much pain you're going through. I'm also keenly aware that you *have* to figure out ways to manage. If you collapse under the pressure of this aftershock, your marriage, family, and future will suffer even more damage. That may not seem fair, but it's true. You and your response are key to moving forward in the best way possible.

Like Paula, you may already have discovered that all coping mechanisms are *not* created equal. Some are healthy and effective, such as counseling, talking with trusted friends, and seeking spiritual support. Others work poorly, producing only temporary results or causing further complications. Unfortunately, too many wives, including myself in the past, opt for ineffective ways of coping.

Distorted thinking can make you feel better for a short time and easily fool you into believing that you're coping well. But ultimately it fails to produce real peace. At first, distorted thoughts enable you to distance yourself from unpleasant feelings, ideas, or behaviors, but sooner or later, your pain and distress will resurface.

That may sound like bad news, but it isn't. Exposing distorted thinking makes room for healthy thinking and effective actions.

Let's examine five kinds of distorted thinking so many women struggle with.

1. Denial

Aiden had given Olivia so many implausible explanations for his suspicious behavior that she could recite them in her sleep.

"Women don't understand men's sexual needs," he said. "I'm a normal guy, okay? I'm fed up with you and your stupid imagination! I'm not doing anything wrong, and you know it!"

Olivia couldn't compete with Aiden's debate tactics. Over time she learned to accept his weak justifications and eventually believed the lies herself. Her girlfriends tried to shake her into reality, but denying the truth was easier for Olivia than facing her fears.

"They don't know Aiden the way I do," Olivia explained when we met in my office. "The pornography on his computer was from a computer virus that planted tempting links in his web browser. He's a strong Christian man!"

Olivia's seventeen-year-old daughter expressed exasperation as she described her dad's undeniable online porn habit.

"I don't understand Mom," she said. "Even when the naked people and disgusting videos were right there on Dad's monitor, Mom made up excuses for him. When I gave her more proof, she said, 'No husband is perfect. We are Christians; we need to forgive.' Dad will never change, and I'm pretty sure he's also having an affair. I wish she would wake up and do something about this!"

Sound incredible? It isn't. The ability to see the best in people and circumstances is an admirable trait, but only if those perspectives are firmly grounded in truth and reality.

As we discussed in the previous chapter, a woman may cling to a childish, idealistic dream of a perfect marriage and ignore glaring evidence of problems. She may view her role as an adoring, supportive wife who excuses her husband's imperfections and forgives his indiscretions.

If you see yourself in Olivia, you may also realize that your denial is driven by innate fears and a desire to avoid unpleasant experiences. This kind of distorted thinking is rife with danger. Over time it will result in more denials of the truth, and you'll become increasingly out of touch with reality. This can lead to full-blown anxiety and even clinical phobias.

Compliantly accepting your husband's deception and lies

may keep your illusion of the happy family alive, but it isn't healthy and will cause more problems the longer you deny the truth of your situation.

The solution is simple but not easy. Choose to be honest, first with yourself and then with your husband. You will likely need to include other trusted and safe members of your family in the conversation as well. It would also be helpful for you to talk with a counselor or spiritual adviser about the best way to navigate any necessary family disclosures.

At this point, disclosing the truth about your situation to your family might be too frightening to pursue. No matter the extent of initial sharing, it's vital to face the truth, be honest with yourself, and let your husband know that you no longer believe his denials.

Stop denying that he's behaving in a damaging and hurtful way. As you come out of denial into reality, you'll find that coping with the truth is much better than believing lies.

2. Rationalization

Abigail wasn't in denial. She had stopped lying to herself years ago, but unfortunately she fell into a different trap—the trap of rationalization.

She knew the truth about her husband's affair, and she was sick of his fabrications and ridiculous justifications. But she made a conscious decision to keep the peace at any price until the children graduated from school and left home. In spite of her husband's adulterous behavior, which had given her a sexually transmitted disease, she told herself that her passive response was virtuous. "It's for the sake of the children," she'd say. "It's the only way to keep the family intact."

Are you caught in a rationalization trap like Abigail's? If so, in your heart of hearts you probably know that your thinking is driven primarily by your emotions. You feel distraught, frozen with fear, and completely at a loss as to how to cope with an out-of-control husband. But rather than admit this to yourself, you rationalize. You come up with a more acceptable and respectable explanation for your lack of initiative.

There's only one way to get out of this rut. You need to be gut-wrenchingly honest about your emotions and motivations. Learn to replace passivity with a productive, godly strategy for confronting your wayward spouse. If you don't know what to do, don't let embarrassment or pride keep you from asking for help. Remember, this is not your fault. No one is responsible for another person's unfaithful actions. It's actually healthy and respectful to draw a caring but firm line in the sand that calls your husband into the process of change.

3. All-or-Nothing Thinking

Wendy's story illustrates another common form of distorted thinking: all-or-nothing thinking.

When Wendy discovered her husband's affair, she was devastated. She immediately jumped to the conclusion that divorce was her only option and considered contacting an attorney to discuss the situation.

"If I don't divorce Brad, I'll be living with this betrayal the rest of my life. He's forever ruined what we had together," she told me one day in tears. "I can't stand the pain. I see no other way to survive. What else can I do?' I think I'm falling out of love with him anyway."

Fortunately there's another alternative for Wendy. She isn't as stuck as she thinks. In our romanticized culture, it's easy to think we must either have the "all" of a blissful, faithful marriage or the "nothing" of divorce.

Living in the throes of aftershock can produce paralyzing fear and block creative, flexible, and realistic thinking. Wendy's mind needed to be transformed and renewed as Romans 12:2 states.

This transformation and renewal takes time and good counsel. Proverbs 15:22 reminds us that "without counsel plans fail, but with many advisers they succeed."

If you feel like Wendy and are contemplating an all-or-nothing plan to survive the aftermath of your own aftershock, wait! You have more choices right now than you can readily imagine. The alternatives may be unfamiliar or require learning a new skill, but they're often the best solution. Seek the counsel of a spiritual mentor, a close Christian friend, or a professional therapist who can help you explore a workable plan you might not have considered yet.

You may feel that your all-or-nothing option is the only one you can live with, but keep reading this book, working through the activities at the end of each chapter, and seeking wise counsel. You might end up changing your mind!

4. Automatic Negative Thoughts (ANT)

Psychiatrist Daniel Amen uses the acronym ANTs (automatic negative thoughts) to describe the pessimistic, cynical, and hopeless thoughts that can plague a troubled person. It's easy to fall into automatic negative thinking, especially when you feel trapped and unable to come up with any practical solutions to your problems. Here are a few classic examples of ANTs[1] or ANT-like thinking:

- *Extreme-ing:* thinking in unrestrained ways ("He's exactly like his adulterous father. He will never change.")
- *Labeling:* attaching a negative label to yourself or others ("I'm an idiot for staying in the marriage with a know-it-all husband.")
- *"Always/never" thinking:* using words like *always, never, no one, everyone, every time,* and *everything* when you think about or describe your situation ("Our marriage has always been broken," or "Nothing's ever been happy for us and no one can help.")
- *Fortune-telling:* predicting the worst possible outcome in a situation ("If I tell him how I feel, he'll divorce me, and then my children and I will be homeless," or "We'll never be able to have good or meaningful sex again.")

The first step in dealing with ANTs and ANT-like thinking is to recognize them for what they are. In your journal, write out the events and circumstances associated with your automatic negative thoughts. Take an objective look at your feelings. Then when you've identified the ANT, *kill* it; in other words, counter the irrational thought with a more accurate and reasonably flexible assessment of reality. You'll be surprised what a difference this simple process can make.

5. Overspiritualization

Sandy was devastated when she got a call from the police station: Her pastor-husband, Kelsey, had been arrested for indecent exposure.

"I was crying so hard," she said, "that I knew I couldn't drive down there by myself. So my best friend, a member of our church, picked me up and gave me a ride. That was extremely kind of her, of course, but on the way to the station, she began offering well-meaning but dismissive and unhelpful comments: 'Kelsey's arrest may be a blessing in disguise. God's at work despite the enemy's schemes to destroy you both. Through your crisis, the whole church will have an opportunity to grow stronger.'"

This type of distorted thinking is called *overspiritualization*. It's hard to describe without seeming to criticize perspectives that, in their proper context, are perfectly legitimate and thoroughly Christian. It's true that there's an unseen spiritual dimension to every situation that confronts us in life, and God is always willing to work redemptively in each one. But problems arise when we turn this truth into an excuse for copping out or refusing to confront the facts. We have to see and face the full reality and context of a difficult situation and the devastating pain we or others are experiencing.

A client I'll call Alexis is a clear example of this style of coping. She came into my office, sat down, and proceeded to tell me about the multiple times over the years she had discovered her husband, Dylan (also an elected official), sexting women on his iPhone. One of those women called Alexis and announced that she was pregnant and Dylan was the father. Then she threatened to contact the local newspaper if she didn't get the money she wanted. The extortion was appalling, but Alexis had a way of distancing herself from her fears. As soon as she finished relating the details to me, she immediately said, "But it's okay, because God makes things turn out well for people who love Him."

As a Christian therapist, I agreed in the broadest sense with her belief in the redemptive character of God, but I also needed to help her understand that she was taking Romans 8:28 out of context. The verse says, "We know that for those who love God all things work together for good, for those who are called according to his purpose."

While it's true that God will eventually resolve all of our heartaches and suffering, that doesn't mean He expects us to deny our human experience by putting on a happy face and simply accepting evil. On the contrary, He wants us to express our thoughts and feelings honestly as we depend on Him for guidance in the midst of our trials.

What's more, there are occasions when He calls us to partner with Him actively in confronting sin and injustice. There are times when it's important to stand up for yourself and fight back.

Alexis was tempted to jump immediately to a spiritual truth without walking through the healthy, though painful, process of facing her husband's betrayal and potential public fall from grace, not to mention the work needed if she chose to restore her terribly broken marriage. Her coping mechanism of over-spiritualizing wouldn't allow her to cope well with the aftermath of her husband's sexual infidelity.

All five types of distorted thinking have one thing in common: they are ineffective for solving your marital problems. If they work at all, their effects are only temporary. They can also be demeaning to you and your mate. And in the end, you're still left without a solution. Like many things in life, the longer something remains broken, the more difficult it is to fix, and secondary problems are created.

This, of course, leads to the inevitable question: If distorted thinking doesn't work as a long-term strategy for coping with your husband's pornography use and sexual infidelity, what does?

In the next chapter, we'll discuss some ways you can take good care of yourself mentally and physically so you can move toward stability and progress in your recovery.

Become the *you* God created you to be. Even in the face of such difficult challenges, He wants you to live a fulfilled life and know the joy of being His beloved daughter. God doesn't promise a life without trials, but He does give you principles to live by that can help you navigate the rough waters of a world filled with disappointments.

As Romans 12:2 says, "Be transformed by the renewal of your mind." Test, or discern, what God's will is for you and your marriage. The process of thinking and discerning takes time, and you need help. That help is with you right now! The powerful love of God will work in your mind and heart as you continue to walk with Him.

When you know you are eternally loved, you can experience hardship without beating yourself up. You can experience pain and still believe that healing is not only possible but is actually happening. You can experience challenges while sensing God's strength flowing through you. All of this is true for your husband, too! And if he happens to be reading these words, I want to say to him, I pray that the profound and unconditional love of the Father will rest upon you—His child, His son. And I pray that God's relentless love will touch your heart as a man and affect your choices for recovery as well. You, too, can be who God created you to be in every area of your life—but you can't do it alone!

REFLECTION
Never be afraid to trust an unknown future to a known God.
ATTRIBUTED TO CORRIE TEN BOOM

QUESTIONS
1. How do you think about yourself in the midst of this aftershock?
2. What thoughts go through your mind as you become aware of how you see yourself?
3. Which kinds of distorted thinking do you most identify with?
4. Are you ready to exchange distorted thinking for the truth?

PRAYER
Father, help me understand how much You love me and how transformed thoughts and behaviors can bless my marriage. In Jesus' name, amen.

CHAPTER 4
TAKE CARE OF YOURSELF

You are my refuge in the day of disaster.
JEREMIAH 17:17

ANITA CAME TO SEE ME after living with the shock of her husband's pornography use for several months. Her emotions had ebbed and flowed since discovering why he no longer seemed interested in sex with her, but she was suffering terribly with the rejection and humiliation she lived with every day.

> I just don't know how to live this way. Watching John act as if nothing has happened makes me furious one day and just plain sad the next. I go through the motions of normal life to keep our three children from knowing that something is wrong. All three are in middle school. I feel like I'm always in the car driving

them to school and activities, or in the house cooking and cleaning, or in my home office between carpool trips.

John and I walk around each other on pins and needles. If I try to talk to him, he gets mad and says he's trying to stay away from pornography sites on his computer, but he still sneaks downstairs to his office when I'm asleep. I know what he's doing, and I just don't understand the pull of images on a machine being more appealing than I am. I've done all I know to be attractive and desirable, but he just isn't interested in me. I keep trying, but he doesn't even notice when I shower, put on makeup, and switch sweats for jeans and a nice top before he gets home to a practically gourmet dinner.

I can keep my cool for several days, and then I'm blasting into his office in the middle of the night raging at finding him on his computer again. I even knocked it off the desk one night and stormed back to bed. I locked the door, and he slept on the couch. The next morning I was sorry I locked him out of the bedroom and started the dance of trying to keep the peace all over again.

Be Responsible for *Yourself*, Not Others

Like many wives, Anita was so focused on John that she totally neglected herself. She spent all of her energy either trying to win his affection or punish him for his behavior. Before she could start to take care of herself, she needed to believe a very important fact: Her husband's behavior was not her fault.

You also need to believe this fact: *Your husband's behavior is not your fault nor yours to fix.*

Many wives go to great lengths to change themselves in hopes of regaining their husband's fidelity. They may alter their physical appearance, their spending habits, their domestic skills, or their performance in bed. Anita tried everything she could think of, but nothing worked. She didn't realize that her thinking was based on the myth that she could change herself enough to restore her husband's faithfulness to her till death parted them.

You could be an absolutely *terrible* wife, and your husband could *still* decide to keep his marital vows. On the other hand, you could be Wonder Woman, and he might *still* betray you. His choices are his responsibility.

Your responsibility is to be the woman God created you to be. And you need to realize that God didn't create you to take care of your husband and everyone else but neglect yourself to the destruction of your own well-being. You are the daughter of the King, the beloved of your Father, the redeemed of the Lord.

You won't feel any of those truths if you're stumbling along regretting or being preoccupied with your passive or aggressive reactions.

That's what Anita was struggling with. But eventually she realized that her reactions of passivity or aggression weren't helping her at all. Exhausted and confused, she yearned for some stability.

Stay Out of the Ditches

The following illustration shows how you can walk through this painful crisis in a healthy way, with stability, faith, and assertiveness. It also can help you avoid the two common mistakes of overreacting and underreacting that I mentioned in chapter 2.

> Ahead of you lies a road that represents the path of a healthy woman walking with the Lord during this part of your life journey by living according to the principles and guidelines that God has given you in His Word. As long as you continue walking on this road, you remain stable. But you need to be careful and vigilant, because deep ditches border both sides of the road.
>
> On the right side is the ditch of passivity. If you fall into that ditch, you live each day trying to keep the peace and not rock the boat. Above all, you are determined not to upset your husband. As a result, you're reticent to confront his destructive actions and attitudes and are seldom willing to stand up for yourself. You convince yourself that your husband's behavior isn't so bad. You are likely insecure and, perhaps, depressed. During a crisis, you revert to a sense of helplessness. You may be a highly competent and confident woman in other areas of your life but still feel powerless in your marriage. Passivity says, "You win. I lose."
>
> On the left side of the road is the ditch of aggression. If you fall into this ditch, you become angry and defiant. You assume your marriage can never be saved. You make up your mind to get tough and do whatever it takes to survive. You want to protect yourself and hurt your husband as much as he has hurt

you. You might see no option but divorce. Aggression says, "I win. You lose."

Some people stay stuck in the ditch of passivity for years. At some point, they may decide they've had enough mistreatment, but rather than make a wise choice, they jump into the opposite ditch of aggression. But once they feel uncomfortable in that ditch, they usually jump back into the ditch of passivity again.

Unresolved fear and anger often lead to this hot-and-cold attitude. These extreme responses accomplish nothing and give the enemy an open door to attack you and your mate.

Between the ditches is a level road called *assertion*. This road is paved with biblical principles that offer hope and healing for you, your husband, and your marriage. As you walk on this road, God will lead you to seek mutual cooperation and partnership. Godly assertion says, "I win. You win." Both you and your husband have the greatest opportunity to see and interact with God when you choose this path.

Hopefully this illustration will help you regain your equilibrium whenever you find yourself sinking into passivity or storming toward aggression.

Wives are often confused about the definition of the word *assertive*. It's not surprising, since our culture often models negative female aggression. On the other hand, the church sometimes teaches a distorted view of submissiveness that looks like passivity in disguise.

Assertiveness means asking for what you want in a manner

that respects others. It is a willingness to speak the truth in love, with confrontation if necessary, as Ephesians 4:15 explains: "Speaking the truth in love, we are to grow up in every way into him who is the head, into Christ."

"Speaking the truth in love" is possible when you are managing your emotions instead of letting them control you. Reining in your emotions is no easy task and takes prayerful practice. Assertiveness can explode into aggression with just one negative response from your husband. Passivity, on the other hand, will resurface if a woman believes there's nothing she can do if her husband refuses to change or seek help.

I've heard many troubled wives recite Bible verses about waiting on God, praying without ceasing, and turning the other cheek as they remain stuck in the ditch of passivity. Of course you want to follow biblical teaching, but reciting Bible verses isn't enough. Godly assertiveness (not aggression) is needed for your marriage to begin healing. If your husband refuses to change or get help, you need to crawl out of that stagnant ditch of passivity and stand firmly on the solid ground of truth, living like the woman of God you are. The best way to survive aftershock is to become confidently assertive. Later in this book, we'll explore in detail what you need to calmly confront your husband in love.

Two classic resources for learning assertiveness are *Boundaries in Marriage* by Dr. Henry Cloud and Dr. John Townsend and *Love Must Be Tough* by Dr. James Dobson.

Practice Self-Care

Women usually underestimate the benefits of self-care, especially when they're overwhelmed as they try to hold their families together. But taking care of yourself is necessary for you to move forward. Only on this stable foundation will you be able to start building a healthier future.

There are many ways to take care of yourself, from something as simple as taking a walk to something that requires more planning, such as taking a trip. In addition to engaging in activities you enjoy, try the following seven self-care steps. They include some mental practices and actions to help you stay out of ditches and practice self-care as you walk with the Lord on a firm and level path.

1. *Develop a support group.* It might seem as if *self-care* and *receiving care* from others are opposites, but they're actually two sides of the same neglected coin. All of Scripture is about relationship: your relationship with God and your relationships with other people.

You desperately need safe and trusted prayer partners *of the same sex* to help you through this difficult time. Because you're extremely vulnerable right now, it's important to avoid leaning on someone of the opposite sex or anyone to whom you might be romantically or physically attracted. Ask for God's help in deciding whom you should trust with your personal and marital information and your feelings. This is a great challenge for many wounded women. They either tell no one, or they tell anyone who will listen, which only adds to their problems.

The depth of friendships varies greatly. You may have friends you enjoy being with, but you wouldn't share personal problems with them. You may also have a handful of friends you've known long enough to trust with some of the issues in your life, but not the most painful ones. Then there are two or three close friends who love you unconditionally and can be trusted to hear your heart without judgment. These friends are there for you at any time, listening attentively, responding with sympathy and wisdom, encouraging you, and hugging you. And if you need a strong word, they'll deliver the truth in love.

When you're too weak to keep walking, these women will come alongside to support you while you regain your balance. They can be trusted with your confidences and will pray for you without ceasing.

If you haven't shared your painful struggle with this small group of sisters in Christ, talk to them today. Let them know what you're going through and ask for their support.

If you don't feel you have any deep relationships like this, talk with a mature Christian woman who might be willing to walk through this with you.

2. *Determine to persevere. Perseverance* is defined as the determination to persist in the face of obstacles or discouragement. Hebrews 12:1-2 (NIV) gives us a vivid picture of perseverance: "Let us run with perseverance the race marked out for us, fixing our eyes on Jesus, the pioneer and perfecter of faith. For the joy set before him he endured the cross, scorning its shame, and sat down at the right hand of the throne of God."

You are in a race you didn't expect, and I imagine that joy seems elusive right now. But here you are. You are at the starting line, in the lane marked "Woman of God." The finish line is far ahead of you, beyond several turns that will challenge your endurance. Healing and restoration await you at the finish line: restoration as a woman who is confidently walking with God—loving Him, trusting Him, following Him, whole in Him and deeply loved—and, perhaps, even restoration with your husband.

"But wait," you say. "The race I was running has turned into a totally different one. I was a godly wife, and then I was betrayed. Now I'm in a race to hopefully restore our marriage *and* myself! How do I run *this race?*"

A still, small voice slips into your mind and whispers, *The same way you ran the other one: by looking at Me.*

Like an athlete who has trained for and run many races, you will live to run again. Yes, you have suffered a severe injury that needs time to heal. You'll have to work hard to rehabilitate and get back in shape to run well again. There will be more pain that will make you want to quit this race. But you are *not* a quitter!

The joy set before you will help you stay in this race, and that same joy will transform your life. No matter what happens after you cross the finish line—marriage restored or not restored—*you* will be whole. If you walk away now, you have little hope that you *or* your marriage will be restored. But if you stay in this race, you have great hope for success.

Your goal is to "run with perseverance the race marked out for [you]." You do this by committing to keep going even when the going feels intolerable. Determine to go all the way to the finish line, following the process that can lead to restoration that I've laid out in this book. Once you've determined to persevere, you can stop questioning whether to keep running this race or quit.

To "keep running" means to keep on reading and engaging with this book, taking time to work through the activities at the end of each chapter, doing the things suggested in each chapter, and trusting the One running next to you the entire way.

This is self-respect, godly determination, and self-care at their best. You can do this! You are on your way.

3. *Pray and act.* "I've prayed and prayed, and Bill isn't changing," Tiffany told me the third time we met.

"Did you talk to him about what you want changed now that he's admitted to an online relationship?" I asked her as she avoided looking at me.

"I tried to. He said he would end it, but to please give him time. I asked a few days later, and he got really mad at me," Tiffany said like a scared little girl.

I asked her what she did then, and she said she quietly walked away and prayed again that God would change Bill.

Praying is an essential part of our Christian lives. And sometimes we are to wait on God for an answer. But at times, we can use prayerful waiting as an excuse not to face something we fear, such as setting a necessary boundary or taking a necessary action.

Tiffany admitted to me later that she was afraid that if Bill continued to be mad at her, he would move out and go live with this other woman. Her fear paralyzed her. The only action she took was emotionally walking on eggshells. And that's no action at all.

Maybe you feel pretty certain there's some action you *should* take, but you're afraid that if you do, it will only make matters worse. Talk with your support group and pray about what to do. Consider what's changed since you found out about your husband's behavior. If nothing has changed, or if your relationship has worsened, it's time for action. Don't make rash decisions, but think about what you've learned so far about your situation and take the wise action you feel led to take.

4. *Intentionally remember the truth.* Without remembering the truth, no problem can be solved.

Pornography is dangerously addictive and damaging—that's the truth. But the urgency of this truth can easily become minimized in your mind if you're repeatedly told that pornography isn't a serious problem.

Your husband's words are powerful and influential, and because of his own shame, fear, and need for the "companionship" of his addiction, he may desperately want to prevent you from turning his pornography use into an issue.

You know the truth, but when he denies or dismisses his unfaithful behavior, he can plant doubts in your mind. You may question yourself again and again as you move through your day. After all, we live in a culture that's saturated with pornographic or near-pornographic images. What's the big deal, after all?

Tragically, you know what the big deal is! You live with the results of your husband trying to believe that a lie is the truth. The lie is that pornography use is no real problem. But here's the truth:

- Pornography and unfaithful actions or flirtations are damaging to your marriage.
- Your self-respecting actions can influence the direction of your marriage and may be the very thing that jump-starts the necessary healing journey. Marriages can be healed.

We help ourselves remember any number of other truths. We write down times and dates of important meetings. We put notes on the refrigerator door and on desk lamps to remind ourselves to let the dog out at certain times. We copy meaningful verses and phrases and display them where we can look at them for encouragement.

Why not do some of those things to help you remember encouraging truths as you practice self-care during this difficult time?

One way to keep truthful thoughts in your mind is to make use of your journal. Write down helpful and encouraging statements so you can refer to them when doubts overtake you. Review those statements regularly. Repeat them to yourself when your husband or other people make comments to the contrary.

You can also set an alarm on your cell phone to go off every few hours as a reminder to silently repeat these truths as you go about your daily business. Write the word *truth* on a sticky note and tape it to the bathroom mirror. That one word is all the prompting you need to remember that pornography is damaging your marriage.

All of these simple aids can help you *intentionally* remember the truth. Truth is the most important weapon in your arsenal. Remember what Ephesians 6:14 (NIV) says: "Stand firm then, with the belt of truth buckled around your waist."

5. *Avoid talking in circles to your husband about his pornography problem.* Amy was stuck. She and her husband, Allan, seemed to get caught in the same conversation over and over again. It would start with Amy trying yet another approach to get Allan to agree to go for counseling.

"I heard about a counselor today who has a great reputation for helping couples," she'd say. "Why don't we make an appointment and see how it goes?"

"You know I don't think we need to do that," he'd fire back. "I hardly ever go on the internet sites you hate. Every guy I know looks at them at least once in a while."

"But, Allan . . ."

"Stop it, Amy. You're nagging!"

And on it would go until Allan would storm off in anger or Amy would dissolve in tears.

Can you relate? If you're reading this book, I imagine you've already been through a lot of discussions like Amy and Allan's. You repeat the same phrases over and over. You hop on the same merry-go-round without ever getting anywhere. There is no resolution. Sooner or later you begin to feel like a nag. You and your husband are caught in a pattern that has both of you spinning in circles.

The process of ending that pattern can begin with you. You have more God-given power in your marriage than you might realize. You can refuse to engage in the same old fruitless dialogue. Step off that merry-go-round and don't hop back on.

All it takes is one person—one spouse—who is willing to stand firm.

Your husband may resist your attempts to alter course, but that doesn't mean you have to give up in defeat. Instead of repeating the dizzying pattern that Amy and Allan's story illustrates, briefly speak to your husband in a way that might sound something like this:

> I know the last time I chose to say something about
> my desire for us to get counseling, it turned out to be
> a hard and unpleasant conversation. I'm not seeking
> to repeat that. But I do owe it to you and myself to be

fully truthful and authentic about the fact that I'm still uncomfortable and concerned about the pattern that's occurred and harmed our marriage. I also think it's right for me to feel this kind of concern.

So I'm making a clear request for you to join me in a counseling appointment I've set up. I made this appointment to begin to learn how to work through where we are in our relationship. Whether you take part or not, though, is fully up to you, and I recognize that. I want to learn how to face these issues differently and create change, preferably with you alongside me. Either way, I'm committed to talking with someone who can offer support and insight, because I desperately want and need it, and I think our marriage does too.

This is my plan, and I want you to join me. The appointment is already set, and I wanted you to know of my decision. I also want to give you the chance to make your own decision. I love you, I love me, and I value our marriage enough to act.

You'll notice the I-based language I used in this example. This approach in sharing your own plan and request will help you keep from hopping on the same spinning merry-go-round. If, however, the attempt to create a brief but productive conversation falls apart, remember that you can calmly step away and get off the merry-go-round. Do so as soon as you can rationally and appropriately create a pause in the conversation and then take yourself elsewhere.

One way you can respectfully exit the merry-go-round is

with a brief explanation. For instance, "I'm going to take a break because I'm not able to be who I truly want to be right now, given my emotions," or "It seems to me that we're starting the unproductive cycle again, which is why I'm going to step away from this topic for now. I'd like to discuss it differently through counseling in the future."

6. *Stop clinging.* "She's a clinging vine" is an uncomfortable and perhaps even offensive phrase used to describe a wife who has trouble standing on her own two feet. However you feel about it, it's not a positive image, but what can be taken from it?

I'm reminded of something that happened when our kids were still toddlers. Like lots of little children, our daughter used to carry a worn-out baby blanket everywhere she went. We were in the middle of a road trip, heading to our next destination, when the ear-splitting sounds of crying and wailing erupted in the car. Wouldn't you know it? The blanket had been left behind at the motel! There was no decision to make: We immediately turned around and went back to retrieve the beloved security rag.

A clinging wife is a bit like a toddler clutching a security blanket. Just as the toddler *needs* the blanket, so the wife can't function without her husband. At least that's how she feels about it. She *needs* him to be near her and assure her that he won't leave her alone. She *needs* to stay married to him no matter what. He is her sole security blanket.

Clinging is a psychological response based on fear. That fear may be connected to anxiety about doing what is perceived to be "right." Women cling because they're afraid that it isn't right to nag, confront, or challenge their husbands. They believe that a good Christian wife never puts her own needs first, and she certainly doesn't contemplate separation or divorce. Fear of financial insolvency can also drive women to cling to the false security of a marriage at all costs. But there's no amount of money that can recompense you for the anguish you're enduring right now.

It's important here *not* to leap to the conclusion that if you give up clinging, it will automatically lead to divorce. In fact, just the opposite is true. Clinging plays a role in allowing the problem of your husband's pornography to stay the same and eat away at you and contributes to the deterioration of your marriage. In psychological terms, it's a form of *enablement*.

Conversely, confronting your husband, speaking the truth in love, and precipitating some kind of crisis can provide just the impetus that's needed to turn things around. In short, the skill you need to develop is *self-respect*. As I've already said, you are a beloved daughter of God. Your security is grounded in what *God* says, not what your husband, your culture, your own thoughts, or your childhood memories keep telling you. So make it your aim to respond to your husband as an adult partner—not a clinging vine but a mature woman—committed to improving your marriage in new ways.

7. *Balance these six self-care steps with caring for your husband.* The steps we've discussed are all about working on yourself: reordering your *own* thinking and changing your *own* behavior so you can become the woman God wants you to be. But God also wants you to love and care for your husband.

Don't misunderstand. I don't want you to equate "care" with old, unhealthy ways of relating that are demeaning to you. Caring means balancing your hurt and disappointment with an understanding that God also loves your husband, and he is potentially able to change with effective help.

The best thing you can do for him at this point is to allow him to see you walk with a healthy self-respect as you also pray for him with godly compassion.

REFLECTION
Review the seven steps in this chapter; then take some time to journal about staying out of ditches. Write about the ditch you seem to fall into the most. What can you do that will help you stay on firm, *assertive* ground?

QUESTIONS
1. Which of the areas covered in this chapter seem the most challenging to you?
2. Identify some of the triggers that engage you in the same old conversation over and over again.
3. What can you do to short-circuit and reroute this reaction as soon as these triggers are pulled?
4. What's something you can do in the next week to begin to respect yourself?

PRAYER
Father, help me understand how much You love me and how changed thoughts and behaviors can bless my marriage. Help me stay on the level road with You, where my real security lies. In Jesus' name, amen.

CHAPTER 5

"WHY DOES HE DO WHAT HE DOES?"

*Can a man carry fire next to his chest
and his clothes not be burned?*

PROVERBS 6:27

"IF I COULD JUST UNDERSTAND," Georgia said as she sat in my office. "Ray is a good man. He does seem to try not to look at pornography, but I know he's still using it. He's depressed and irritable and sometimes misses days at work after spending several hours a night in his home office viewing pornography on his computer. What can I do? I can't wrap my head around it."

Georgia is not alone. Many wives believe they would be able to move through their aftershock better if they understood why the grip of this damaging behavior on their husbands seems so strong.

Two Reminders

As you read this chapter, you must continue to believe that *your husband's choices and actions are not your fault.* Understanding why your husband does what he does is very helpful for restoring your marriage, but the reasons for his behaviors should not become excuses for their continued presence in your marriage.

It's also important to remember that while this chapter and book focus on pornography use, there are numerous other sexual or emotional "symptoms" that can and do occur apart from pornography use. Various types of damaging habits or behaviors can be tied to the root issues talked about in this chapter.

Stopping pornography use alone, whether it's a long-term or short-term "sobriety" that's somehow managed, doesn't typically address what's under the surface. Those deeper issues are looked at in this chapter, and they're why internet filters, bouncing the eyes, and behavior modification through sheer effort never fully and redemptively transform a life and marriage.

How It Begins

Early Exposure

"Do you have long-term problems viewing pornography from magazines, the internet, DVDs, adult entertainment clubs, or something else?" I asked Matthew, the husband of a couple I was counseling.

"Well, I can manage to avoid those things," he said. "But when I was twelve, my cousin showed me a black-and-white photo of a naked woman. I never seem to forget it. That event and image are engraved in my brain and run through my mind in various ways all the time. It's my mind and fantasy that completely control me."

Matthew's early trauma with all of its mixed emotions (shame, interest, fear) had sealed this image in his brain in such a way that it controlled his thinking and resulted in addictive patterns.

Another man, also the husband of a couple I was seeing, had a very serious problem with pornography and was desperate to find victory. He didn't hesitate for a moment when I questioned him about the origins of his obsession.

> I was six, and it was the month of June. My dad was a pastor, and my parents had invited a visiting missionary to spend the night at our house. When I emptied the guest-room trash the following morning, I came across a *Playboy* magazine in the wastebasket. From that moment, I knew I would be in love with those pictures for the rest of my life.

This man had innocently come across an image as a child that remained in his mind into adulthood and paved the way for addictive pornographic behavior. The emotional climate of his upbringing was a perfect environment that isolated him with this sexual secret and caused the images to become a confusing yet soothing excitement for him.

Lack of Connection, or Intimacy Disorder

In an online TED Talk titled "Everything You Think You Know about Addiction Is Wrong," author Johann Hari explains that the opposite of addiction is *real and caring* human connection.[1]

The term *intimacy disorder* is another way I describe a deep and pervasive lack of connection. Here's what I mean: An intimacy "disorder" is a stunted ability or emotional pattern that makes it difficult to establish close, authentic, or vulnerable relationships. This condition not only limits a person's ability to have empathy for others and connect emotionally with them on a day-by-day basis, but it can also affect the sexual relationship with one's spouse. In some cases, the varied interpersonal challenges associated with intimacy issues may meet the criteria for diagnosable mental-health conditions known to strongly affect relationships, including social anxiety, attachment disorder, and various personality disorders. However, individuals without these diagnosable conditions can also experience intimacy problems. That's why it's important for you and your spouse to see a well-trained professional who can look at the whole picture. But remember that understanding the root issues or diagnoses associated with certain sexual behaviors and symptoms doesn't excuse your husband's actions. However, it can enable you to move toward help and solutions.

A number of factors likely contribute to your husband's sexual behavior, but quite often, at the root is difficulty with intimate connection. Intimacy problems can affect your husband sexually, as well as emotionally and spiritually. Because God made us to thrive and grow in connected, safe relationships, when things go awry relationally, a deep personal shame sets in. Toxic shame whispers in a person's head, *I'm bad. I'm unworthy. I'm unlovable.*

From these feelings of badness or personal filth come various ever-present forms of self-protection that skew a person's self-esteem and view of life. It's not hard to imagine how this way of living inhibits healthy intimacy and leads to disordered or false intimacies; that is, fleeting but "safe" escapes and substitutes for intimacy, such as pornography or prostitution. Of course, these lustful escapes are anything but "safe," yet to an individual who feels threatened or insecure with being vulnerable and deeply known, they provide a sinful cocoon of "false safety" since no emotional demands or true personal sacrifice are placed on them by these forms of so-called pleasure.

Abuse and Neglect

Matthew was the fourth child in a family of seven kids. His parents were good people who loved all of their children. Matthew was also a shy little boy. By the time his three younger siblings were born, Matthew had pretty much given up trying to be noticed. He was obedient, so he wasn't scolded, but he also wasn't noticed in positive ways.

The same was true at school. Other kids weren't mean to him. They just didn't pay much attention to him. He got decent grades and played intramural basketball when he entered middle school. After a game, the other kids usually joked around in the locker room without including him. But one day, a few of the guys were looking at something they'd all pulled up on their smartphones. One of the popular boys noticed Matthew staring at them in all the commotion.

"Hey, Matt, come here," the boy yelled to him.

"Look at this," his teammate said as he directed the screen of his phone toward Matthew.

The image of a nude young woman blazed before Matthew's eyes. He could feel the heat crawling up his face, and an uncomfortable smile invited more interaction with the other guys.

"Whaddya think? Pretty good, huh!" his teammate beamed as he slapped Matthew on the shoulder.

It felt good to connect with guys who had ignored him for

years. And then there was that image. Matthew didn't have to see it on the phone screen again. He had it firmly in his mind. *But why not look at it on my own phone?* he thought.

Matthew was hooked. He sat before me now, a married man with two children of his own. He had never realized that the unintentional social neglect he suffered as a child negatively impacted him to this day. Pornography was a regular part of his life and was hurting his marriage to the point that his wife was threatening separation.

There are two kinds of damaging sins that others can inflict on us when we're young, impressionable, and vulnerable: (1) sins of *commission*, also known as *abuse*, and (2) sins of *omission*, otherwise known as *neglect*. We're aware of the many abuses children suffer, but we seldom hear much about neglect.

Matthew's parents were doing what they thought was right, but they overlooked this quiet, compliant child. They neglected to affirm him, praise him, and validate him.

Your husband may seem a bit like Matthew—the quiet type, unlikely to cause trouble, compliant with many of your wishes, except for his pornography problem. Your husband's parents might not have been intentionally unkind, and you may be very kind and affirming as a wife. But if your husband *is* like Matthew, the emotional neglect he perceived in his childhood set the conditions for pornography to feel affirming and exhilarating and to offer him what seems like a helpful escape into a positive world.

Unfortunately, unless abuse and neglect are discovered and their victims experience healing and restoration, the impact of these damaging sins can linger well into adulthood.

Abuse and neglect can be divided into five categories:

physical, sexual, emotional, verbal, and spiritual. At this point, we've been talking only about men, but both men and women may have been subjected to abuse or neglect as children.

You or your husband might have endured one or more of the following kinds of abuse or neglect:

	Abuse	Neglect
Physical	Hits, slaps, mistreatment	Unmet basic needs, touch deprivation
Sexual	Inappropriate touching, rape, incest	Lack of godly sex education
Emotional	Intimidation, mind control, manipulation	Absence of love and bonding
Verbal	Name calling, criticisms, insults	Lack of affirmation and validation
Spiritual	Hellfire threats, religious manipulation, feeding toxic guilt/shame	Withholding God's grace and redemptive path

It's important to understand that abuse and especially neglect can be extremely subtle in nature, almost to the point of escaping the victim's conscious attention. Also, children who have been abused or neglected hardly ever blame the adults in their lives. They blame themselves. They grow up thinking, *There must be something wrong with me.*

Matthew found acceptance from the other boys on the intramural basketball team when he joined them in their locker-room antics. Pornography became a source of good feelings. When he was alone at home, he could shut himself in his room and look at images on his phone or computer. No one would even notice. Now his marriage is being damaged by the same ingrained coping mechanisms.

Accessibility

Past generations compartmentalized pornography use into a male habit, or maybe an innocent activity of young, single men. Those preconceptions were quickly shattered early in my career as a sexual addiction therapist.

I spoke with a set of parents on the East Coast who sadly reported the grim story of their six-year-old, Anna, who had recently started crying every night before falling asleep. Eventually they discovered that her anxiety came from watching internet pornography.

"I can't stop looking at videos on Daddy's computer!" she told them through her tears.

That same week I talked with a father and mother from the West Coast. Their normally compliant first grader, Xavier, had begun misbehaving at home and disrupting his classroom. The parents and school counselor were determined to understand this sudden change in his personality and formulated plans to help him, all to no avail.

Xavier's behavior grew worse and worse until at last he went to his older brother and begged, "Take away those naughty pictures in my mind!"

It's easy to see how the internet has entirely altered the pornographic landscape by making obscene materials widely accessible, affordable, acceptable, and anonymous. It would be fair to say that present-day pornography bears little resemblance to the material available prior to the invention of the World Wide Web. In the past, gaining access to pornography was challenging. Users who needed a fix had to find some pretext for leaving the house at night and then drive to an adult bookstore or video store, hide their car in a dark alley, and do their best to sneak in and out of the store undetected. Consequently, the onset of addiction tended to be gradual. That's not the case anymore. The rapid availability and increasing novelty of pornography alter the brain's natural, God-given sexual response in profound ways.

Your Husband Is the Target of a Huge Industry

Over the past twenty years, an explosive expansion of internet technology has taken place, providing instant access to explicit sexual sites. As a result, the onset of addiction is more rapid and can become full-blown within a surprisingly short period of time.

Pornography is frequently the precursor or gateway to sex addiction, since internet pornography impacts individuals of all ages and cultures, regardless of personal background, education, or socioeconomic status.

The problem is immeasurably compounded when the viewers' brains aren't yet fully developed—in other words, in children (like Anna and Xavier, as well as your husband if he encountered early exposure), adolescents, and young adults under the age of twenty-five. The younger the viewer, the more traumatizing the pornographic encounter, both mentally and physically. This sets up youth for even more intense and dangerous addictive behavior in the future.

You may feel discouraged after reading this, but don't lose hope! I've said it before, and I'll say it again: You, your husband, and your marriage can be healed and restored.

Answering the question "Why does he do what he does?" will give you some perspective on the challenges your husband faces. And hopefully it will encourage you and your husband to get help from a therapist who specializes in sexual addictions.

Why Is It So Difficult for Him to Stop?

Logan had no idea he was addicted to pornography. This was odd, since he sometimes spent hours at night in front of the computer watching and masturbating to one pornography video after another, each time seeking one more tantalizing than the last. Sometimes, even though he didn't exactly plan to, he'd watch videos all night long until he was completely exhausted.

"I feel so tired the next day, it's unbelievable," he said when he finally came to the point of acknowledging his problem and seeking my professional help. "It's really hard to focus on work. I stare at the computer screen and feel numb. I don't want to be around anyone, and I get irritated very easily. I'm exhausted after a binge, but I can't fall asleep because my mind is so wound up. I can't eat, and it's like I'm only half there, just a shell of the man I could be. I can't stand to look in the mirror. I have zero libido after my marathons, and no desire to associate with real women, especially my wife. I hate to see that look on her face when she suspects I'm bingeing again. All I feel is guilt, anxiety, and anger at myself, but I take it out on her to get her off my back. Then I feel terrible, but it gets worse! That's when I panic, desperately craving my next fix. The very thing I hate but like to do for relief is what I find myself doing again."

Although the details and intensity vary from person to person, a cycle similar to Logan's is common for men who want to stop their pornography habit yet feel it's impossible to resist.

"WHY DOES HE DO WHAT HE DOES?"

Let's consider two key reasons why your husband may find it difficult to stop using pornography. And remember, *insight* and *information* are not *excuses*, but they may help lead to a more effective strategy and pathway out.

1. *Pornography is addictive.* According to the dictionary, an *addiction* is a physiological or psychological dependency upon "a habit-forming substance (as heroin, nicotine, or alcohol) characterized by tolerance and by well-defined symptoms upon withdrawal." If you know anything about drug addiction and withdrawal symptoms, you might be thinking that Logan sounds a lot like a man trying to break free from a heroin or cocaine habit. If that's your reaction, you're right on target.

In many critical ways, using pornography and illicit drugs are variations on the same theme because they both activate the same area and neurochemistry of the brain.

Over the past several years, an abundance of research consistently demonstrates that even moderate pornography use creates changes in the human central nervous system. "The central nervous system consists of the brain and spinal cord. The brain plays a central role in the control of most bodily functions, including awareness, movements, sensations, thoughts, speech, and memory."[2]

Why does your husband have a difficult time stopping his behavior? Because science has shown us that actual physical changes take place in the brain that perpetuate an addiction. Sexual addiction occurs when a person feels a strong compulsion to repeatedly engage in certain behaviors, such as pornography use, even at the expense of his or her own physical, mental, relational, or financial well-being.

2. *The brain makes stopping complex.* "Are you trying to convince me that Nicholas has a brain problem so I'll just forget that he gave me an STD? Are you siding with him?" Jocelyn demanded. "He tells me all the time that I should take the antibiotic and quit griping. Now I'm supposed to be happy that he's only doing pornography and not going to prostitutes."

I let Jocelyn express her frustration and then replied, "I'm sorry you think I'm siding with Nicholas. My intent is not to excuse or justify his betrayal in any manner. At the same time, I'm attempting to help you realize that solving Nicholas's sexual compulsions is more complex than simply focusing on his clearly sinful and immoral behavior. His problem is in body, mind, and spirit."

During a crisis, it's understandable that you want to focus on the hurtful actions of your spouse. You don't want your therapist to let your wayward husband off the hook. I hope by this point, you trust that is not my intent and will accept the fact that we need to face the entirety of the problem to achieve healing for both of you.

The science involved in brain research is complicated and hard for the nonscientists among us to comprehend, so I'll just focus on one example.

One of the most promising medical developments that has been gaining attention over the past two decades is SPECT scans, imaging tests that reveal overfunctioning or underfunctioning parts of the brain. According to psychiatrist Daniel Amen, who has performed more than 70,000 of these scans,[3] SPECT is a useful tool for diagnosing and treating complex cases of sexual addiction.[4]

Amen believes that "a SPECT scan helps patients develop a

deeper understanding of their problems" and see them "from a medical point of view," which can "dramatically decrease shame, guilt, stigma, and self-loathing. Scans also help increase self-forgiveness and the forgiveness and understanding of others. Patients can see that their problems are, in part, a medical problem and not simply 'willfulness run riot.'"[5]

I'm not suggesting that your husband go out and get a SPECT scan. Neither am I saying that brain science explains away sin or negates accountability in the marriage or to God. I just want you to know that science is researching addictions, and the results may help you and your husband overcome a challenging obstacle to his victory over pornography use—which is a sexual sin affecting the body and brain (1 Corinthians 6:18). Another positive indicator from brain-science research in recent years is that with time and investment, the brain can and does change and heal.

Hopefully this information about the brain will help you realize that your husband's behavior isn't just a habit he can easily stop. But the good news is that research-revealing truths about how people function often result in answers to questions like "Why does he do what he does?"

And answers can help fuel healing and restoration.

Signs of Addiction

Ilene's friend had been encouraging her to talk to me. Ilene smiled warmly as she shook my hand and then sat down. She explained that she probably didn't need to see me at all, but her friend kept bugging her about it, so she made an appointment.

"I've wondered if my husband has an addiction to pornography," she began, still smiling. "He has told me that he struggles with it, but that it's no big deal. I probably talked too much to my friend, but I just needed to process with someone."

I asked her what she was experiencing that led her to talk to her friend. She went on to describe a number of changes she had seen in her husband that caused her to wonder if he was hiding something from her. After listening to her for almost an hour, I told her that her husband did show some signs of a man who is likely struggling with a pornography addiction but may not fully perceive the extent of his problem.

You might be wondering the same thing. Does your husband display any signs of an addiction to pornography or some other sexual compulsion? Read the following list calmly and consider whether your husband is displaying any signs of addiction. (Note that the term *user* refers to a person who is using pornography.) These signs may not describe your husband at all. But even if they do, there is help available for you and for him.

1. *Compulsion.* The user experiences an uncontrollable drive to access pornography or engage in illicit sexual activity.

2. *Negative shifts in personality, behavior, or habits.* When addiction takes over, it can have dramatic negative effects in multiple areas of the user's life, including decreased productivity at work; relational problems leading to divorce and family breakdown; alienation of friends and family; changes in eating and sleeping habits; reduced attention to personal hygiene; risk of STDs and/or unintended pregnancy; increased shame

and loss of integrity; and the potential for legal problems and arrest as the behavior becomes riskier and more deviant.

3. *Continuation despite negative fallout.* Despite the consequences, the user continues indulging in the behavior to satisfy his sexual appetite.

4. *Obsession with planning or obtaining sexual experiences.* Preoccupation with his sexual compulsions is so powerful that the user can't stop thinking about it. The longer the pattern persists, the more the person will neglect important duties and priorities to have more time, money, or energy for sexual activity.

5. *Compromised marital intimacy.* The user may sometimes engage in sex as a means of escaping intimacy rather than increasing intimacy with a spouse. The interpersonal aspect of sex is forgotten as it becomes an impersonal, mechanical means of achieving a high. As in drug addiction, more sex and increasingly deviant sex are required over time to achieve the desired effect. Ultimately, sex is regarded merely as an act of self-satisfaction rather than an act of mutual giving, serving, and sharing between spouses.

6. *Sexual dysfunction.* The user may experience sexual problems, including erectile dysfunction; inability to maintain an erection without self-stimulation, pornography, or sexual fantasy; premature ejaculation; delayed ejaculation or inability to ejaculate; less satisfying orgasms; loss of libido; or sexual awkwardness.

7. *Physiological and psychological symptoms.* The user may experience other physiological and psychological problems, including anxiety, chest pain, chronic fatigue, high blood pressure, loneliness, depression, suicidal thoughts, incoherent speech, or insomnia.

8. *The use of lies and deception to hide impulsive behaviors.* Shame, loss of self-respect, self-loathing, or fear may compel the user to cover his tracks to avoid detection.

9. *Inability to quit.* The user's exhausting attempts to stop his behavior may include the following:

- Changing residences in hopes of starting over
- Initiating new relationships with the intention of controlling the problem—this time
- Breaking off *all* sexual relationships, only to give into his sexual compulsions again
- Repeatedly making and breaking promises to himself and others
- Switching to a different addiction as a way of compensating (the average addict has at least two addictions)

In the end, all of these efforts prove futile.

A Biblical Perspective

Hebrews 12:1-2 (NIV) offers a biblical perspective on addiction: "Since we are surrounded by such a great cloud of witnesses, let us throw off everything that hinders and the sin *that so easily*

"WHY DOES HE DO WHAT HE DOES?"

entangles. And let us run with perseverance the race marked out for us, fixing our eyes on Jesus" (emphasis added).

Although the Bible doesn't use the modern-day term *addiction*, God has much to say about entangling and addictive behaviors. Addiction to alcohol is probably the best example. In the Jewish culture, drinking wine was a common practice at social events. Wine was also used for medicinal purposes and had other practical applications in daily life. In every case, the potential for using it to excess was always present.

As a result, there are numerous places throughout the Bible where the Lord clearly confronts excessive use of and dependency on alcohol (see, for instance, Proverbs 20:1; 1 Timothy 3:3, 8; and Titus 1:7; 2:3). Paul admonishes us not to overindulge and get drunk with wine, which will ruin us, but rather to be filled with God's Spirit (Ephesians 5:18). We can safely assume that this principle applies to *anything* that is harmful to people and destructive to their relationship with God, including inappropriate drug use, gluttony, inappropriate sexual activity, and pornography.

When people become addicted, they compulsively or habitually focus on a substance or behavior that eventually controls them. This is a form of idolatry. The Lord speaks plainly in the Ten Commandments against idolatry and says that we are to have no other gods besides Him (Exodus 20:3-4).

The Bible also instructs husbands and wives to remain faithful and keep the marriage bed healthy, active, and "undefiled" (1 Corinthians 7:5; Hebrews 13:4). Marriage should "be honored by all" (Hebrews 13:4, NIV), and pornography use does just the opposite.

You Are Here

Now that you understand how formidable the opposition really is, we're ready to move forward into the light of a new hope.

Sometimes learning the science behind a man's behavior can seem overwhelming to some women, but remember, there is nothing too difficult for God. By His grace, there is no problem that cannot be overcome. In fact, many people in the most caring and Christ-centered addiction support groups say that their closeness to friends and Jesus came *because* of their presence in an intimate, accepting, and nonjudgmental environment of care.

I want you to hear that with proper support, treatment, and motivation, your husband can lead a healthy, highly functioning life, and you can have a fulfilling marriage. The first and most important step is acknowledging the problem and then seeking God's divine help through wise relationships. Bring others close during this season of need and recovery!

REFLECTION

Find a smooth stone and write this verse on it as a reminder of God's faithfulness: "Then Samuel took a stone and set it up between Mizpah and Shen and called its name Ebenezer; for he said, 'Till now the Lord has helped us'" (1 Samuel 7:12).

QUESTIONS

1. How would you answer the question, "Why does your husband do what he does?"

2. After reading this chapter, how important do you think it is to find out whether your husband has symptoms of addiction? Why?

3. How will your response to your husband change (or stay the same) now that you've learned that his sexual compulsions are, in part, a biochemical problem and, as Daniel Amen wrote, "not simply willfulness run riot"?

4. If you're inundated with thoughts of giving up or feelings of despair, how might you combat Satan's lies and continue to believe God's truth?

PRAYER

Heavenly Father, I want to understand the reality of my husband's struggle, but I am struggling too. Help me turn to You for help rather than turning inward and dwelling on my overwhelming circumstances. Enable me to see my husband from Your perspective so I can pray for him according to Your will. In Jesus' name, amen.

CHAPTER 6

MAKING DECISIONS AND PREPARING FOR ACTION

[I pray] that according to the riches of his glory he may grant you to be strengthened with power through his Spirit in your inner being, so that Christ may dwell in your hearts through faith—that you, being rooted and grounded in love, may have strength to comprehend with all the saints what is the breadth and length and height and depth, and to know the love of Christ that surpasses knowledge, that you may be filled with all the fullness of God.

EPHESIANS 3:16-19

Karen's Story

Vince sat in my office, head down, hands fidgeting, and tension radiating off him like a heat wave. Karen was explaining why she and her husband were seeing me for counseling.

Several weeks before this day, Vince had admitted to Karen that he had been using pornography for years and had continued to ever since they married a year earlier. He told her that he had thought it was no big deal, so he didn't mention it to her before their wedding. Now it was eating him up with shame and guilt. He knew it was affecting their relationship because of his increasing hesitancy to initiate sex with Karen.

She was shocked and hurt. They tried to work things out on their own but realized right away that they needed help. Even with Vince's sincere repentance, he knew something else besides using pornography was going on inside him, and he quickly agreed to get help.

Tami's Story

"My husband has been involved in some sort of pornography—mostly movies—for as long as I can remember," Tami confided to me. "We've been married for eleven years, and he's now taking a men's class to help him overcome this issue. In spite of this, he's not getting better. I feel like I still need some extra help. How am I supposed to respond when I come home or get up in the middle of the night, and he's watching pornography and masturbating? Should I just be quiet and turn away? Or should I actually say something to him right then? This has been happening about once every few weeks for years.

"Last time, I said, 'Why are you still doing that?' He, of course, was embarrassed and said he was sorry, but yet he acted kind of mad. As his wife, I love and support him and want to encourage him in his walk with God, but I'm not sure what to do in this situation."

Lynne's Story

"My daughter won't talk to me anymore," said Lynne, "and it's all because I'm still living with her dad."

I was listening to an incredibly sad story. Lynne and her husband had been married for twenty-one years and had three beautiful girls. Two of them had already left the nest. The youngest was still living at home when Lynne finally decided to

MAKING DECISIONS AND PREPARING FOR ACTION

reach out for help. By that time, it had been eight years since the middle daughter had accused her father of sexual abuse. The case had gone to trial, but because of a legal technicality, Lynne's husband had been acquitted. The three girls didn't agree with the court's ruling. In fact, the older two daughters were so frustrated that they cut off all ties with their parents.

What made Lynne's story especially tragic was that she had *known* about her husband's problem with pornography, cybersex, and sex addiction for a long time.

In the beginning she had nothing to go on but a strong suspicion—an unsupported intuition that something was terribly wrong. He denied it, of course, and accused her of being paranoid whenever she broached the topic. So she dropped the subject and waited. After all, she didn't want to rock the boat or create difficulties for her children. She didn't want them to end up feeling abandoned or fatherless. Unfortunately, by the time she had more evidence and made up her mind to act, it was too late. The damage was already done.

"There's no doubt about it now," she said when she contacted me for counsel. "It's obvious what he's been up to, and I'm afraid for the daughter who is still living with us. He continues to deny everything and makes up all kinds of weird excuses as to why pornographic websites are showing up on his phone. I'm so confused. Is it time to leave? Is there any hope that he might change? Or has he gone too far for me to remain in our marriage?"

What's Your Story?

Karen's husband, Vince, revealed his pornography use to Karen within their first year of marriage. He agreed to get help and cooperated with everything he needed to do to restore his marriage.

Tami's husband still struggles with using pornography even though he's attending a class to help him stop. He is making some attempts to change but isn't gaining ground in his recovery.

Lynne's husband was acquitted of sexually abusing one of their daughters and for years has consistently denied having a problem with pornography, cybersex, and sex addiction. He flatly refuses to own his actions or get help.

If you're like Lynne and Tami, you've already confronted your husband about his behavior, but no real change has occurred. If your story most resembles Karen's, you have the foundation and initial actions on which to restore your marriage.

Some of my female clients admit they make snap decisions based on emotional impulses without weighing the options or considering the consequences. But most of the wives I counsel are just the opposite: they're apprehensive and a bit weak-kneed whenever the subject of decision-making is brought up.

I was in the latter group when I faced one of my bigger crises. I was scared and had put off making a decision about my circumstances for way too long. After losing much sleep one night, I got out of bed to ask the Lord for help and opened my Bible to the book of Hebrews. My eyes fell on a verse I didn't recall reading before: "Therefore lift your drooping hands and strengthen your weak knees, and make straight paths for your feet, so that what is lame may not be put out of joint but rather be healed" (Hebrews 12:12-13).

I immediately remembered a doctor looking at an X-ray of my foot years before. He pointed to the X-ray and said, "That little bone there was broken a long time ago. Apparently you never took care of it, and that's why your joint hurts now."

As I focused on the verse in Hebrews, I saw the connection. I was scared and weak-kneed. I wasn't taking care of my crisis. The longer I remained undecided, the worse my situation would become. God was showing me that it was time to make a decision and act on it.

I've not only been where you are now, but I've counseled many women who have been there too but have walked the path of recovery and are enjoying the fruit of their courage. Marriages have been restored, and even if they have not, these women have grown into the people God intended them to be. If they could talk to you right now, they would encourage you to stop living in an unwittingly self-defeating way. It isn't healthy for you, your husband, or your children. And it's not what God wants for any of you.

Understand the Severity of Your Situation

In chapter 5, I shared how various root issues including lack of caring human connection or intimacy disorders can explain why some people are lured into using pornography. In some cases, the addictive nature of pornography and destructive sexual behaviors carry severe complications and cause extensive damage to both partners and the marriage.

To assess and treat the underlying and varied conditions, a more specialized type of counseling is needed in lieu of traditional counseling.

Traditional counseling is probably the kind of counseling you're most familiar with. Perhaps you've tried this route in the past, meeting once or twice a week for fifty-minute sessions with a general marriage counselor or your pastor. Traditional therapy is effective for broad-spectrum marriage issues, such as when a couple has a fairly good foundation but has hit a serious snag. Think of it like going to your family physician. In a given week, he or she treats a wide array of issues, from a sore throat to a broken leg, and maybe delivers a baby. However, if your family physician suspects that you have throat cancer, he or she will send you to an oncologist. The physician understands that your condition could be extremely serious, requiring a specialist with years of additional training and experience.

Intensive marital counseling is, in my opinion, a more ideal approach for couples who suffer with an intimacy disorder and the other root issues which are typically part of sexually addictive behaviors. They need a marriage specialist with additional training and expertise in treating complex relationship symptoms. The specialist not only treats the surface behaviors but also knows how to assess, diagnose, and treat the bigger issues hidden beneath the surface. Treating these deeper core issues or "drivers" of the sexual compulsion requires a different format—several hours or blocks of time over three to five days in a row. Couples are usually quite surprised when they discover that several months' worth of therapy is accomplished in one week, and it truly changes the direction of their lives and marriages! Obviously, one week of therapy isn't a complete magic fix, but think of it like a surgical procedure or radiation treatment for a marriage in crisis.

Continue Focusing on Self-Care
The goal of this chapter is to lead you to the important step of deciding to confront your husband about his sexual behaviors.

MAKING DECISIONS AND PREPARING FOR ACTION

Perhaps you've already confronted him many times, but he hasn't changed. This time, your confrontation will be different.

Before we explore what that looks like, let's revisit an important self-care step from chapter 4: The first step in caring for yourself is to develop a support group. If you haven't done that yet, begin working on it right now!

Here are some other good reminders from that chapter:

> The depth of friendships varies greatly. You may have friends you enjoy being with, but you wouldn't share personal problems with them. You may also have a handful of friends you've known long enough to trust with some of the issues in your life, but not the most painful ones. Then there are two or three close friends who love you unconditionally and can be trusted to hear your heart without judgment. These friends are there for you at any time, listening attentively, responding with sympathy and wisdom, encouraging you, and hugging you. And if you need a strong word, they'll deliver the truth in love.

The other six steps are important too, but developing a support system is essential for you right now. You need the love, support, and encouragement of a committed group of friends as you face one of the most challenging decisions of your life.

Make a Decision to Confront Your Husband

You are now at a critical juncture in this book . . . and in your life. I know these are strong words! But I don't take lightly what I'm going to ask you to do.

You need to make a decision to confront your husband. Specifically, you need to ask him to

1. acknowledge that he needs help, and
2. agree to treatment that fits his situation.

Maybe you're thinking, *I've already asked him to do these two things a dozen times, and he just refuses to change. We go right back to where we've been all along.*

But this time you'll be asking in a different way and allowing your husband to experience natural, logical consequences if he refuses to get help. (We'll talk in more detail about consequences in chapter 7.) This will be a serious conversation that can accurately be described as a loving but firm and unwavering confrontation.

And this time you've finally reached the place where you're ready to stop living with the pain and degradation you've endured. You've been working through the activities at the end of each chapter and taking seriously the lessons learned in the process.

I don't know you personally, but I do know that if you've gotten this far in the book, you're ready to stand up and take a positive step that can motivate real change in your marriage. By now you're well-informed and can make this decision with confidence! You've grappled with the aftershock of your husband's actions, worked on understanding your own emotions and distorted thinking, recognized the importance of self-care, and learned a great deal about the power of addiction and why your husband does what he does. (At this point, I'm assuming you've said "yes" to practicing the skills emphasized so far and are ready to move forward with your decision to confront your

MAKING DECISIONS AND PREPARING FOR ACTION

husband. If not, spend some time reviewing the work you've completed so far and asking God to give you the courage you need for whatever steps He's leading you to.)

If you're ready to choose the path I'm recommending, the rest of this chapter (and the next) will take you from this decision point through

- your husband's response,
- your response to him, and
- into the attitudes and actions that can help you both move toward a restored marriage.

As you move ahead with your decision and prepare for action, I pray . . .

> that according to the riches of his glory [God] may grant you to be strengthened with power through his Spirit in your inner being, so that Christ may dwell in your hearts through faith—that you, being rooted and grounded in love, may have strength to comprehend with all the saints what is the breadth and length and height and depth, and to know the love of Christ that surpasses knowledge, that you may be filled with all the fullness of God.
> EPHESIANS 3:16-19

I affirm you and your character for making this difficult decision, and I pray that God will grant you all of the power and love that is yours in Him. No matter how you feel, God is at work, and He is with you!

Next, we'll cover some important guidelines you need to understand and follow *before* you confront your husband.

Anticipate Your Husband's Response

Your husband's response to your specific requests will determine what you do next. The purpose of anticipating his response is to help you avoid being shocked and losing your composure. If you get rattled at this point, you might not be able to go any further.

The stories of Karen, Tami, and Lynne illustrate three possible ways your husband will respond when you confront him:

- *Possibility 1:* He will show interest in more fully understanding your felt concerns, express sorrow for his actions, and demonstrate a desire or willingness to get help.

- *Possibility 2:* He will vacillate, make excuses, or back away from any definite course of action.

- *Possibility 3:* He will flat-out deny that he has a problem and will refuse to cooperate in any way.

These possibilities will come into play in the next chapter when you actually see and hear your husband's response.

Weigh Concerns of Domestic Violence

Another vital issue I want you to carefully review and consider in light of your marital history is any risk of domestic violence upon confrontation. If physical risks or retaliation of any kind are present, and especially if history in the relationship confirms this, you must seek counsel before any direct confrontation. Only do so in a location and overall manner that does not place yourself in danger.

Do not proceed with confrontation if this is part of your marital dynamic until you have full outside support and safety measures in place. Holding this conversation with the awareness of another person, and potentially in a public and visible location, can be key.

I *emphatically* note to you this directive and concern. Listen to your instincts and wise counsel, and do not dismiss any clear risks or even nagging concerns you hold concerning your physical safety.

Learn to Discern Worldly or Godly Sorrow

When you confront your husband and he notices that you are now confident and have a calm and self-respecting determination he hasn't seen before, he may initially show sorrow over his hurtful behavior. You may have heard his contrite words before and grabbed hold of them in the desperate hope that they were sincere. But time and his failed promises proved otherwise.

There is a difference between worldly sorrow and godly sorrow. Worldly sorrow is primarily self-centered and exclusively consequence driven. If your husband has shed tears or displayed grief simply because he was caught in the act, or because his own sin has caused him pain, that's worldly sorrow. Indications of worldly sorrow include the following behaviors:

- He fails to back up his words with specific, decisive, and visible actions—along with empathy.

- He promises to take part in counseling but backs out at the last minute, or he starts therapy but drops out, covering his retreat with all kinds of empty excuses, such as "We can't afford it," "I know more than that counselor knows," or "I don't have time right now."
- He makes all the right gestures but continues headlong in leading a secret life riddled with sexual sins or affairs.
- He reverts to the same old deceptions the moment he's told that he's forgiven, and his remorse evaporates.

If you see these signs, you can be fairly sure you're dealing with worldly sorrow, not genuine or lasting remorse, because your husband shows no empathy for another person's pain and isn't sorry enough to make a serious investment in changing.

In the next chapter, you'll learn how to respond differently when he expresses worldly sorrow than you have in the past. Hopefully, a changed response on your part will result in a changed spouse and potentially a changed marriage.

Godly sorrow often produces positive results as soon as your husband's behavior is revealed. You may be blessed with a husband who chose to tell you immediately when he realized he had a pornography or sexual addiction. Or perhaps as soon as his sexual compulsions were exposed, he told you the entire truth without holding back any secrets. Some husbands are truly repentant; they're remorseful with a godly sorrow, eager to mend their ways, and ready to cooperate and seek treatment. If that describes the man in your life, your road to recovery won't be nearly so rough.

Create a List of Non-negotiables

The following three non-negotiables will help you clarify exactly what you're requiring your husband to do if he wants to show that he's truly repentant and serious about getting the help he needs to stop his damaging behavior. These non-negotiables are the bottom-line measure of what your husband must accomplish if he truly wishes to restore and heal your marriage.

You can gauge the genuineness of his repentance and his willingness to fully commit to a recovery process based on whether he actively complies with all three non-negotiables.

The Three Non-negotiables

1. *He must implement immediate boundaries to prevent easy access to pornography.* Your husband needs to demonstrate initiative and good-faith efforts to distance himself from his sources of temptation and cut off easy access. While he may have limited insights on what this entails, he needs to produce an initial list of boundaries and observable practices that will prevent him from acting on his compulsions, and then he needs to immediately implement these boundaries. Following are some examples:

- Downgrading or giving up his smartphone
- Using his laptop computer only in common areas
- Installing filters and/or accountability software
- Closing social media accounts, sharing passwords, and changing phone numbers
- Cutting off sinful or risky relationships by engaging in accountable, observable communication that ends the entanglement or affair

2. *He must share his struggle with other men who will hold him accountable.* Fighting this battle alone is *not* an option. It not only perpetuates the isolation and shame that fuel sin and addiction, but it also fails to provide the accountability your husband needs.

Although your husband might not know where to turn at first, he must identify two or three safe and trusted men (your pastor, wise friends, caring siblings) who agree to meet with him on a regular basis for accountability and support. He must reveal his problem to them, as well as the process he's undertaking at this stage. He must also give you access to these individuals so you can verify that he's taken this step and is having regular conversations with them in the days and weeks ahead.

Eventually your husband will take part in a recovery *group* of some kind, which is another step to expect from him. As harrowing and impossible as this may seem to a man new to recovery, a well-run recovery group (one that focuses on emotional skills and transformation, not just behavioral control) can become one of the best and most helpful aspects of a man's growth and his ability to overcome shame and habitual acting out.

3. *He must seek out and begin specialized counseling.* It's minimizing, prideful, and unwise for your husband to insist on dealing with complex sexual issues through self-help alone. Habitual pornography use and sexual sin have underlying roots and causes that can't be solved by simply trying harder and promising to stop. This kind of pain on both sides of the marriage deserves well-informed and compassionate attention. Seeking out and participating in specialized, Christ-centered professional counseling is essential for individuals and couples who

are struggling with the damaging effects of pornography use and sexual sin.

It may seem hard to find this kind of help, but your husband can begin by researching how the process works with various counselors and/or support groups (even if they seem difficult to access). While you should also become familiar with the various routes into counseling, your husband should be responsible for gathering the information needed to set up initial conversations as well as phone and office appointments, and then determine options for proceeding. In the end, both of you should take part in this process. It's also ideal if both of you have individual as well as marital support.

Along with these non-negotiables, insist on a counselor or support group that specializes in sexual addiction or pornography use in marriages and has ample experience with these issues. General, nonprogrammatic counseling without some specific process for addressing pornography and/or sexual addiction integrated into it is insufficient, and it often unwittingly allows the problem to become worse.

Resources and referrals that can help you and your husband with these non-negotiables can be found by contacting Focus on the Family's Counseling Services Department online at FocusontheFamily.com/Counseling or by calling 1-855-771-4357. You can also find helpful links and content by exploring the "Family Q&A" web page at FocusontheFamily.com/FamilyQuestions.

Don't worry about trying to absorb all of this information now. It's a lot to take in all at once, so you can imagine it will be a lot for your husband to take in as well. When you get a counselor involved, he or she will be able to help both of you apply these non-negotiables in a reasonable time frame.

But have your list of non-negotiables ready to go. I'd also recommend printing a copy you can give your husband. If he acknowledges that he needs help and agrees to treatment that fits his situation, then you can present the actions he must take if he wants to restore your marriage.

If your husband fully and willingly undertakes these actions, there is great reason to hope that it will lead to positive change and deeper healing for him and your hurting marriage.

Be Ready to Share "A Man's Invitation to Recovery"

Your husband may be very skeptical about this book and my advice to you. I hope you'll tell him about my coauthor, Geremy Keeton, who wrote a message to you in the introduction. Assure your husband that Geremy is a highly qualified therapist who has counseled many men and couples who have struggled with issues similar to the ones you and your husband now face.

The following message from Geremy is addressed to your husband. It may be helpful to give it to your husband after you confront him.

A MAN'S INVITATION TO RECOVERY

> *From*: Geremy Keeton, licensed marriage and family therapist and counselor for men
> *To*: The husband of the reader of *Aftershock*
>
> As much as this book is for women, I want you to know it's very fairly written. It's not aimed at bashing

MAKING DECISIONS AND PREPARING FOR ACTION

or shaming you, but it does explain what it takes to restore and renew a marriage. You have an opportunity now to change your marriage for the better! You can step up and be the man you were created to be.

Because I've come alongside husbands who've progressed through recovery and now enjoy the fruits of a transformed life and marriage, I can attest to the fact that it's both hard work *and* worth it.

There are few things more beautiful and positively contagious than a redeemed couple! Although this is likely the furthest thing from your view right now, you can have joy and freedom—for yourself and your marriage. Do you want that? It's your turn to show it.

Similarly, it's your wife's turn to face her own recovery and growth in a healthy way. She must respond to her pain in a self-respecting and measured manner as she watches for what you will do. In large part, your actions over time determine how she can proceed and what she'll decide about the marriage.

I'm urging you to recover not only for her sake but also for *yours*. Your most prized possession as a man is your integrity. You can regain this. If you focus solely on your wife and "performing" to regain her and your married lifestyle, then you will almost certainly falter in your recovery. The days when she's most upset with you, the days when she doubts you because she has flashbacks of pain—these are the days you may temporarily throw in the towel and binge on sinful choices and acting out. If she's not happy and this recovery process is so difficult, you may wonder, *What's the point?* You must learn to answer this question with *sincere self-motivation* and your own pursuit of personal integrity and wholeness.

The fact is, an imperfect journey to full recovery is more common than a perfect one. This complicates things. Counselors and nearly any man in an honest recovery group will agree with that. Fortunately, a marriage can usually weather a slip or imperfection if there are sincere and visibly proven efforts to establish full recovery. That's one reason why self-motivation for your own *personal* betterment (underlying a simultaneous battle for your wife's heart) is so essential. It will help sustain you both through the normal peaks and valleys you encounter on the path to restoring your marriage.

Your wife can feel the difference in your motivation and will most often weather any stormy patches that arise if she sees that you're committed to yourself and your recovery in a healthy way. Her ability to tolerate imperfections along the bumpy road to recovery is especially likely if she feels a growing intimacy and emotional availability in how you share honestly with her about your recovery and the actions you're taking.

Come what may for your marriage, the path of personal health and integrity is always best. No one owns your integrity and walk with God but you. You have a life to live—and if you hope to live it with your spouse, then embracing a strong self-motivation and internally driven hunger for healing is the most likely way to accomplish that.

MAKING DECISIONS AND PREPARING FOR ACTION

REFLECTION

Take some time to journal about the following steps you've taken or will take now as you prepare to confront your husband:

- Understand the severity of your situation.
- Continue focusing on self-care.
- Make a decision to confront your husband.
- Anticipate your husband's response.
- Learn to discern between worldly and godly sorrow.
- Create a list of non-negotiables.
- Be ready to share "A Man's Invitation to Recovery" with your husband.

QUESTIONS

1. Why is it necessary to confront your husband in a loving but uncompromising way?

2. How would you describe your feelings right now? Take time to journal your answer.

3. Do you have a support system of a few friends in place? If not, make it a priority to develop one.

PRAYER

Father, I've made a decision to confront my husband and now ask that You will make your presence known to me as I move ahead with what I believe to be Your will for my life. I thank You for Your love for me and for my husband. Please protect me and give me inner peace and strength when doubts and fears assail me. Give me the power of Your Holy Spirit. Amen.

CHAPTER 7

CONFRONTING YOUR HUSBAND

Rather, speaking the truth in love, we are to grow up in every way into him who is the head, into Christ.

EPHESIANS 4:15

IF YOU HAVEN'T ALREADY DONE SO, it's time to confront your husband with what you know or suspect. The material we've covered in the previous chapters has laid a strong foundation and equipped you to face this task.

If the facts are already in the open, but your husband is taking no solid action to change or address the issue, it's time to confront him with your new understanding of what must happen next.

As you anticipate this confrontation, you might feel like Janet:

> Janet woke up with a knot in her stomach. She was planning to confront her husband, Danny, about his sexual behavior—again. This time, though, she was

ready to confidently ask him a two-part question that would determine the course of their marriage. Depending on how he answered, Janet would move forward with a response Danny hadn't heard from her in the past. A number of things might happen at that point, but Janet was now prepared to handle them firmly and calmly.

That morning Janet spent some time with the Lord and prayed for His will to be done in this confrontation. After a few minutes, she picked up a folder containing two documents that she was prepared to give to Danny at the appropriate time: "The Three Non-negotiables" and "A Man's Invitation to Recovery."

The night before, Janet had asked Danny to set aside some time in the morning to talk with her. He agreed and was waiting for her at the kitchen table, uncertain of what was coming. *Janet seems different*, he thought as she calmly sat down opposite him and put a folder on the table between them.

"Danny," Janet said, folding her hands on the table in front of her, "I have something important to say."

It's Time to Confront Your Husband[*]

By now, you've hopefully talked with your support group and printed copies of the three non-negotiables and Geremy Keeton's message for your husband. You've also anticipated three possible ways he'll respond when you ask, "Are you willing

---

[*] I'm going to repeat the same vital issue mentioned in Chapter 6. As you determine when and how to proceed, you must review and consider any risk of domestic violence. It's only time to confront your husband if you know that any such concerns are clear and accounted for in your plan.

to acknowledge that you need help, and do you agree to get treatment for your behavior?"

Let's revisit these possibilities and how you can respond.

Possibility 1: How to Respond If He Repents and Wants Help

If your husband expresses sincere remorse for what he's done, there's a good chance he might be willing to take a brand-new approach in response to your concerns.

Let's assume that Danny, in the previous story, responds with godly sorrow and repentance. This is when Janet would express the need for specialized pornography-recovery counseling, ideally including intensive marital therapy to thoroughly help their relationship on their healing journey.

How might she do that, and what could she say? Here's one way she might respond:

> Danny, I'm so grateful that you take responsibility for your behavior and you're willing to get help. I've been reading this book called *Aftershock* and have studied the material intensely. It's written by two marriage therapists who specialize in helping couples like us.
>
> What I'm going to suggest now is based on their expertise and the success they've seen with couples who have followed through with their commitment to a thorough recovery plan. I think it would be really helpful if you would read the book too, but even if you choose not to read it, I've decided to take the healthy actions I've embraced after learning from this material. It's a new day for me, and I hope it soon will be for you, too.

I've made a copy of a list of non-negotiables from the *Aftershock* book. This other document is a copy of a special letter to you from the male coauthor, who is an experienced and caring counselor to men. It's called "A Man's Invitation to Recovery."

After you read both documents and absorb the content, we can move forward with finding a counselor.

Obviously, you'll want to personalize this script to reflect the way you talk. You'll also want to be assertive rather than aggressive in your response. Remember the ditch illustration in chapter 4? Make sure to stay firmly on the solid ground of assertiveness and avoid the ditches of passivity and aggression.

From this point, it's a long but direct road to healing and restoration. After your husband agrees to take action on the three non-negotiables, you'll begin the counseling process, both individual support and intensive marital therapy. Eventually, when you and your husband are ready, you'll begin ongoing follow-up care and continue with your recovery plan. This journey won't be easy, but it will be well worth it.

The chart on page 121 illustrates the path you're on.

Possibility 2: How to Respond If He Makes Promises but Keeps Returning to His Damaging Behavior

Helen confronted her husband, Jim, about three months earlier. He admitted that he'd been meeting a woman from his office for lunch for more than a year, and when Helen questioned him further, he also admitted that he and the woman were having an affair.

At the time, Jim had promised Helen that he would break

Action Plan
(Depending on Your Husband's Response)

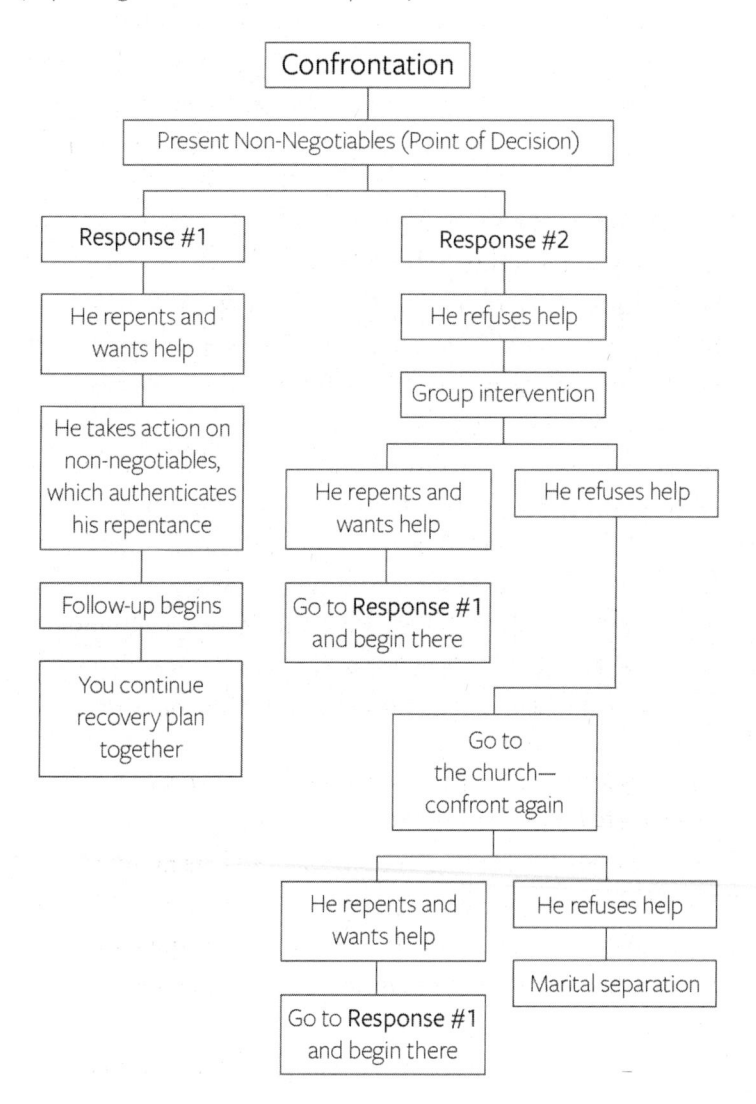

```
                        Confrontation
                             │
          Present Non-Negotiables (Point of Decision)
                     │                │
              Response #1         Response #2
                     │                │
            He repents and        He refuses help
             wants help               │
                     │          Group intervention
            He takes action on        │
            non-negotiables,    ┌─────┴─────┐
            which authenticates He repents  He refuses
            his repentance      and wants   help
                     │          help           │
            Follow-up begins      │            │
                     │       Go to Response    │
            You continue    #1 and begin there │
            recovery plan                      │
            together                           │
                                         Go to the church—
                                         confront again
                                          │          │
                                  He repents   He refuses
                                  and wants    help
                                  help           │
                                    │      Marital separation
                              Go to Response #1
                              and begin there
```

121

off the relationship completely and just be superficially friendly with the woman at work. So Helen gave him another chance.

When Helen's doubts remained, she checked Jim's computer one day while he was at work and found emails between him and the same woman. They were concrete evidence that Jim had broken his promise of ending his emotional and physical infidelity.

Helen was devastated. She had previously been through the painful discovery of Jim's pornography use, and Jim had promised to stop that time, too! But he hadn't, and Helen had decided just to live with her pain over that betrayal.

Now she realized that she should have been stronger years ago. Jim's pornography use had escalated into an affair. He might have tried to stop his damaging behavior, but his good intentions weren't enough to produce true transformation and results that would restore their marriage.

At this point Helen needs to decide how she'll respond to Jim's broken promises and lack of true repentance.

If you're like Helen, and your husband has continued his damaging behavior with no overall progress or trajectory toward health and "sober" living, now is the time to pull in some additional resources and stage an intervention. The input of other people your husband respects could have a significant impact that motivates him to change. The process of staging an intervention and confronting your spouse in this way is a challenging but necessary line in the sand.

To help you prepare for an intervention, you may want to seek professional advice or consult websites for suggestions on how to go about it. I prefer the biblical model from Matthew 18:15-16:

If your brother sins against you, go and tell him his fault, between you and him alone. If he listens to you, you have gained your brother. But if he does not listen, take one or two others along with you, that every charge may be established by the evidence of two or three witnesses.

A formal intervention affirms the serious nature of your husband's sin. It also demonstrates that your complaints are valid, and resolution can only be achieved through penitent actions on his part.

There are two key steps you need to take in staging an intervention.

1. *Select and meet with your two to three key intervention support people.* The first step to take in an intervention is to meet with a small group of people who love and care about you and your husband. The individuals you choose from might be siblings, parents, adult children, friends, coworkers, wise church elders, or employers. This meeting should take place without your husband present, so it might be best to gather at one of their homes. In addition to the primary qualifications of loving and caring about you and your husband, these individuals need to clearly understand that you are doing this in an effort to save your marriage, not to seek revenge by revealing his secrets to others.

Unfortunately, wives often hide the husband's double life from close friends or minimize it so that no one knows what's actually happening. This may mean that the key people in their lives need to be told the *whole* truth for the first time ever.

They may be shocked initially, or you may find that more

people than you realize already know or suspect the truth. Some of them may even know more than you know about your husband's activities. While this might not surprise you, it could strike a painful blow to your heart. Keep a close watch on your emotions during this time and continue taking responsibility for healthy self-care. Also make a mental note to talk with your support group about your feelings.

The preintervention meeting typically requires about sixty to ninety minutes for the people on your team to get facts straight, discuss the need for specialized or intensive marital therapy, and agree on a specific time and place for the intervention.

It's extremely important that each person on the team cares enough about your husband to present a united front with others and be willing to follow through with check-ins and further confrontation if needed.

2. *Carry out the group intervention.* You could handle the logistics of the intervention any number of ways, but here's one example:

> Gail had made certain that Chuck would be home on a particular night. He had planned to watch a baseball game, and she knew he would probably keep to that schedule.
>
> When the doorbell rang around 7:00 p.m., Chuck ignored it as he sat glued to the television. Gail opened the door to greet the people she had pulled together for this group intervention. They gathered quietly in the living room while Gail went to get Chuck. He'd heard the rustling at the door and met her as she entered the family room.

"Who was that?" he asked.

"Come on in the living room, Chuck," she said as she turned to rejoin the others.

Chuck was surprised and confused.

Like Chuck, your husband will probably be surprised and confused if you begin the intervention the way Gail did. You and your team can decide the best way to proceed initially, but what happens afterward depends entirely on your husband.

The purpose of this intervention is to talk to him in a clear, loving, and respectful way about his destructive behavior. Throughout this meeting, the focus should remain on your husband and the specific steps you're asking him to take for healing. Don't let him change the subject by pointing the finger at you or anyone else.

Your immediate goal is for him to agree to the treatment plan. You or the members of your team may already have thought through the details, including scheduling tentative dates with a counseling specialist, lining up childcare, and arranging transportation. If you haven't nailed down the logistics yet, you can let your husband know that it will be done as soon as possible.

Ideally the treatment should begin sooner rather than later. Your husband might come up with a dozen reasons treatment isn't possible. For example, he may claim that he doesn't need help, that therapy costs too much, or that he can't get off work this time of year. Don't be surprised if he partially consents to treatment in front of everyone and then withdraws his consent later. He might even revert to minimizing your concerns and resisting change. This is predictable in some ways because one part of him may want to stop his compulsive habit, but another part of him can't let it go. He doesn't want to lose his security, his escape, his comfort, his mistress, or any other need he thinks his compulsion will satisfy.

To counter his excuses, you and the rest of the team may find it helpful to think in terms of a medical crisis. If your husband were suddenly in a critical accident or diagnosed with a rapidly advancing cancer, then somehow, someway all the peripheral stuff would become secondary, and you would make sure he got the help he needed. If your husband does admit he needs help and agrees to get treatment, you'll follow the same process I outlined for Possibility 1. Be very specific about the action plan and timeline your husband needs to implement.

However, if your husband continues to refuse treatment after the intervention, follow the guidelines in Matthew 18:17: "If he refuses to listen to [others], tell it to the church." This means bringing the problem before the church leadership, and possibly the congregation.

Clearly, this is a radical tactic, since it causes the sin to become generally known and brings to bear the influence of the church. If appealing to your larger church community has the desired effect and your husband agrees to cooperate, you can implement the action plan for Possibility 1, which ideally includes intensive marital therapy. But if your husband remains resistant, there's only one truly helpful option left.

Possibility 3: How to Respond If He Denies That He Has a Problem and Refuses to Cooperate in Any Way

Evelyn sat in the chair in the guest bedroom of her home. She had stopped sleeping in the same bed with Bob after he refused to give up his "casual" emotional flirtation with a woman he met online.

"Her name is Shelly," Bob had snarled when Evelyn confronted him eight months earlier. "She means nothing to me. It's just a fun meeting every once in a while. I've worked like a dog for decades to give you this gorgeous house and trips to Europe, not to mention putting our kids through expensive colleges, and now I just want to have some freedoms of my own."

Evelyn could hear his speech echoing in her brain over and over as she stared at the numbers on the digital clock: 3:00 a.m. How many sleepless nights had there been since she first confronted Bob? Too many to count.

She had screamed, cried, become quiet, read books, talked to close friends, pleaded with Bob, begged to know why this was really happening, prayed, and seen a counselor, but nothing had softened Bob's heart. Instead, he insisted that he didn't need help because he didn't have a problem.

Evelyn had asked a few of the men close to Bob to try to talk some sense into him, but he almost laughed in their faces. Even going to their pastor hadn't lessened Bob's resolve to keep meeting Shelly every few weeks—not to mention viewing underwear models on his smartphone late in the evenings.

Evelyn's adult children knew what their father was doing and could see their mother crumbling before their eyes. They encouraged her to think of herself and tell their father to get out of the house.

The clock clicked over to 4:00 a.m. Evelyn was still sitting in her chair, thinking. She knew that if she told Bob to leave the house, they could end up divorced.

Maybe not, she thought. But she knew she needed to be prepared for that possibility if they separated.

"This is where I am," Evelyn said aloud to herself. "I see that I really can't go on this way, or I'll end up sick and miserable for the rest of my life."

For the remaining hours of the night, she wrestled with her thoughts as she considered demanding a structured separation. Around 6:00 a.m., she startled and realized that she had dozed off. As she walked to the kitchen to get a cup of coffee, a strong and confident Evelyn had emerged to face this day.

Bob came stumbling down the stairs an hour later and started to pour himself a cup of coffee. Evelyn confronted him before he walked out front to get the newspaper.

Two days later, Bob moved out of the house.

An intentional and planned separation as a final test to see if the marriage can be preserved is a bold and biblical step. I would never suggest this option lightly, but Matthew 19:8 makes just such a provision: "[Jesus] said to them, 'Because of your hardness of heart Moses allowed you to divorce your wives [or husbands], but from the beginning it was not so.'"

This verse doesn't specify separation, but I am suggesting a structured separation to test the situation before any conclusion that divorce is the only option in the face of your husband's unrepentant infidelity and abandonment of his vows.[*] Your actions will bring him to a point of decision.

God didn't design marriage so that damaging sexual thoughts and behaviors would be welcomed in and allowed to destroy the

---

[*] For remarks about the question of divorce in the face of pornography use alone, see Focus on the Family's question-and-answer "Pornography as Grounds for Divorce?" at focusonthefamily.com/family-qa/pornography-as-grounds-for-divorce/.

union He ordained. But sin entered the Garden of Eden, and it enters our lives. It can cause the hardness of heart Jesus spoke about in Matthew 19. Yet Christ never fails; He is always ready to soften and heal even the hardest heart.

If you've tried all the suggested actions in this chapter, and your husband still denies that he needs help and is unwilling to seek treatment, only one helpful option remains if you want your life to change for the better: *You must seriously consider the ultimatum of separation.*

I don't know the specifics of your situation, and even if I did, I couldn't tell you what you should do. I've tried to clearly lay out the realities of living with aftershock and the steps you can take to move toward healing, growth, and restoration and become the healthy, self-respecting woman God created you to be.

Having said that, I recognize that the decision to separate from your husband is between you and God. You need to spend time with Him, praying, listening, reading Scripture, reflecting, and trusting that what you conclude is from Him. If you do these things, the power of the Holy Spirit will guide you.

It's possible that an ultimatum will grab your husband's attention in a way that nothing else has. An ultimatum carries with it a consequence.

Instead of saying to your husband, "We are at an impasse, and you need to move out," you would say, "Either we deal with this by getting counseling together beginning right away, or you will have to look for another place to live until you're ready to help resolve this problem."

You can certainly hold on to the hope that your husband will agree to the necessary steps when faced with the reality of a separation. A temporary separation may be just what it takes to open his eyes to the seriousness of his actions and stimulate some badly needed self-examination. Until he's forced to confront a strong consequence, such as separation, he may never find the motivation to change.

But be prepared to follow through on your stated consequence if he still refuses to change. And keep in mind that he may refuse to move out of the house.

If this happens, you may have no choice but to move out yourself. Before you pack a bag and leave, however, make sure that your support system is in place, that people are praying for you, and that you actually have a place to stay, such as the home of a friend or family member.

Let your spouse know where you can be contacted and make it clear that you will be ready to resume negotiations as soon as he is willing to reciprocate. Additionally, if a separation endures for any length of time, it's important to prepare a structured marital separation plan or contract that can be documented. A good counselor can help you with this. Your contract should include clear expectations regarding finances, visits, notifications, and specific boundaries around romantic or emotional entanglements that will further compromise the marriage. The goal is to set a cast for healing the broken bones in your marriage. You don't want to haphazardly cause more damage!

What Do You Do Now?

If your husband expresses true remorse for his actions and demonstrates a willingness to get help (Possibility 1), you are on the road to recovery together. Move on to the next chapter!

If he vacillates, makes excuses for his behavior, or backs away from taking concrete action (Possibility 2), you're probably planning a group intervention or a meeting with your pastor or leaders at your church in the hope that he will finally listen and agree to get help.

If he flat-out denies he has a problem and refuses to cooperate in any way (Possibility 3), he has either moved out or you've moved out and are living elsewhere.

Whatever your situation is, I want to urge you to concentrate on taking good care of yourself. Continue counseling (or start counseling if you haven't yet) and stay close to the body of Christ. If you have children, include them in a healthy, caring community and arrange counseling or mentoring support for them as needed. Don't let financial considerations get in the way. If you think you can't afford professional therapy, think again. Christian counselors know what the current economy is like, and some may be willing to make various adjustments. People just like you are taking advantage of their services every day! I understand what it's like to worry about money, having been in your shoes myself. But I can testify that the Lord is more than able to provide *everything* you need as you put your trust in Him.

I'm going to be especially insistent that you seek *individual* counseling and prioritize self-care. I'm driving home these points and the truth of God's love for you because I know how easy it can be to lose sight of these things. Fact is, you've been hurt. Deeply. You might be grieving the death of everything you had expected and hoped for in your marriage.

You're in the darkness, up against a mighty foe. I know where you stand, and I can tell you that women in your position generally need well-informed and specialized care, as well as time to recover fully. I want you to make sure that you get that kind of godly professional care so you can move forward into the light.

Is Your Husband Aiming to Follow Christ?

Obviously, everything I've said up to this point is based largely on the assumption that your husband is a believer or has been involved to some extent with a church. If this isn't the case, it will make a significant difference in the way you deal with him—hopefully even opening the door of faith for him through this painful crisis.

Even if he hasn't accepted Jesus or sought to model his life after biblical morals, he *has* made a vow or promise to you in this marriage. On that basis alone, and out of your own faithfulness to Christ, you can confront him and call him to what's best for him and your marriage by reminding him of the life you both dreamed of sharing together as a married couple at the beginning.

Gathering people your husband respects and loves to support you in an intervention is still a fitting and wise step to take. It can be done with firmness and clarity, as well as with the godly kindness that is "meant to lead . . . to repentance" (Romans 2:4).

If your husband is a nominal believer whose commitment is wavering, he should be challenged to step decisively toward his Savior. Remind him that what God says about sex and marriage is radically different from what our culture says. If he's still undecided about his commitment, he needs to make up his mind where he stands. Your own willingness to state your personal commitment to Jesus—without badgering him with self-righteousness—can be a gracious witness to him in this hour of decision in his life. He should also make it clear what he wants to do about your marriage.

If he *does* claim to be a committed Christian, it's time for him to revisit his self-professed value system and give some careful thought to what it means to put faith into action. But even if he doesn't, you're right to state that your expectation is for sexual faithfulness and a commitment to work on the marriage, and if he doesn't agree, he has the power to walk away.

When you confronted your husband, you gave him a copy of Geremy Keeton's message, "A Man's Invitation to Recovery." You might encourage your husband to read these challenging words from my coauthor again, with special attention to the matter of integrity.

What If He Never Repents?

Sadly, some husbands may choose to stay willingly stuck in unrepentant sexual sin. While a separation plan can and does activate the great redemption available to a wayward spouse who will embrace it, the fact remains: A husband can permanently refuse to renounce (perhaps even pridefully nurse) the connection with his sin. This may become obvious either by his words or his long-demonstrated actions.

Scripture is the clearest about how you can respond to unrepentant physical infidelity if that is the stark reality you're facing. Divorce is a concession God's Word overtly lays out when a hard heart manifests itself in unrepentant physical infidelity.

Likely more complex, however, is biblically discerning what the course of the marriage looks like if perpetual, volitional, and unrepentant pornography use alone is the case. To be fair, there may be varied theological conclusions, but simply standing by and "making peace" with pornography's devastating presence is not one that my coauthor and I could endorse.

What I can say with all confidence is that in *either* scenario, a person needs *wise pastoral care* combined with *sound professional therapy* and *discernment over an extended period of time*. In other words, any conclusion to divorce is not one to rush, adopt without close counsel, nor eagerly enact as a "simple solution" to the pain that sexual sin inflicts. But for some, this may indeed be the conclusion they arrive at due to the headlong choices a spouse repeatedly makes, proving their long-term, willful, and covenant-violating hard heart.

If, when, and *how* to release someone to the rebellion they have chosen is again a matter of wise biblical counsel and something a wife's closeness to God and His Spirit must guide. In even the darkest valley, there will be provision and the presence of the Always-Faithful One who "sticks closer than a brother" (Proverbs 18:24). If you find yourself at such a crossroads, remember that your *own* health and recovery still remain vital and entirely possible with God. *Victim* is not your identity; *overcomer* is!

REFLECTION

> I call heaven and earth to witness against you today, that I have set before you life and death, blessing and curse. Therefore choose life, that you and your offspring may live.
>
> DEUTERONOMY 30:19

QUESTIONS

1. Is self-care during very hectic and trying times something you've seen other people model in your life? What did they do that would be useful for you to remember right now as you confront your husband? How was Jesus an example of this when He was pressured on all sides?

2. How do you feel after reading this chapter? What do you fear? What gives you hope? Spend time writing about your emotions in your journal.

3. What's the *one* next practical and helpful step you need to plan for and take based on this chapter? Who can best help you?

PRAYER

Father, be "my light and my salvation." With You as my guide, "whom shall I fear?" (Psalm 27:1). I *need* and deeply desire to feel Your embrace and have Your wisdom in every decision. I pray for this both for myself and my husband, whom I know You deeply love as well. In the name of Jesus, my path to You, amen.

CHAPTER 8

THE ROAD TO RECOVERY

*I will restore to you the years that the
swarming locust has eaten.*
JOEL 2:25

*If anyone is in Christ, he is a new creation. The old
has passed away; behold, the new has come.*
2 CORINTHIANS 5:17

AT THE OUTSET, I want to remind you that your own road to recovery continues and is possible even if your husband refuses to repent and your marriage ends.

Continue with the love and redemption of God in your life and in your personal counseling journey. You're not consigned to lifelong pain or a second-class discarded status. You are as you always have been—a beloved daughter of God.

If hope is dawning for your marriage, pursue it! If not, continue in healthy growth for yourself. New paths are ahead even if your husband chooses not to come along.

Fortunately, for Tom and Patsy, marital hope was dawning:

After years of hurt and turmoil over Tom's pornography use and online sexting, Patsy staged an intervention with a few of Tom's good friends.

Broken and repentant, Tom agreed to all that the healing process required, including intensive counseling with a specialized therapist. He and Patsy spent a week away from home at the intensiv\e and came back ready to begin the hard work of restoring their marriage. They understood that the road would be long and rocky and would require many changes in the ways they related to each other.

But Tom was truly repentant and committed to the follow-up plan and group meetings that the counselor had set up for him. Patsy was also working with a counselor who would continue helping her move through the recovery process.

Part of what Tom and Patsy learned in intensive counseling is covered in this chapter. These principles will also help you and your husband move forward as you begin a new way of life.

While this book is primarily written to wives, it would be helpful if you and your husband read the remaining chapters together, especially since it will take *both* of you to accomplish full marital healing.

You may feel exhausted and overwhelmed at this point, but please remember that you are not alone. Your support groups, your counselors, your spiritual community—and most importantly, God—are with you.

No matter how you feel—afraid, doubtful, angry, distrustful—go to your heavenly Father and bring all your cares to Him. This is crucial. The enemy will be nipping at your heels and your mind. Continually go sit with the Lord and shore up your spiritual resources.

You and your husband are at the point of a possible breakthrough right now. I've witnessed possible breakthroughs become reality for many couples who have been where you are. Hang on to hope and keep choosing to follow through with what you know to be true.

Find encouragement from the promises of Joel 2:25 and 2 Corinthians 5:17, which are listed at the beginning of this chapter. Write these verses on index cards and tape them on your bathroom mirror so you can see them first thing in the morning. Post them on your refrigerator door. Put them on your desk next to your computer and stick them on the dashboard of your car. Encourage your husband to do the same.

Remind yourselves that you are two people beloved of God. Draw on that love! It, and He, will help you both.

The Three Bowls

On this road to recovery, the journey toward healing can seem like an endless, confusing maze, and it's easy to lose sight of the process as well as the goal. The diagram of three bowls on the next page is designed to help you visualize where you're heading and how you'll get there. This illustration shows *forgiveness*, which leads to *reconciliation*, which in turn leads to *restoration*.[1] As the bowls progressively nest inside each other, they become a single unified stack.

The arrow at the top of the illustration shows an ingredient being poured into the bowls. That ingredient is *trust*. Restoring the trust in your marriage is foundational to your healing, so we'll take a closer look at this ingredient before we continue discussing the three bowls.

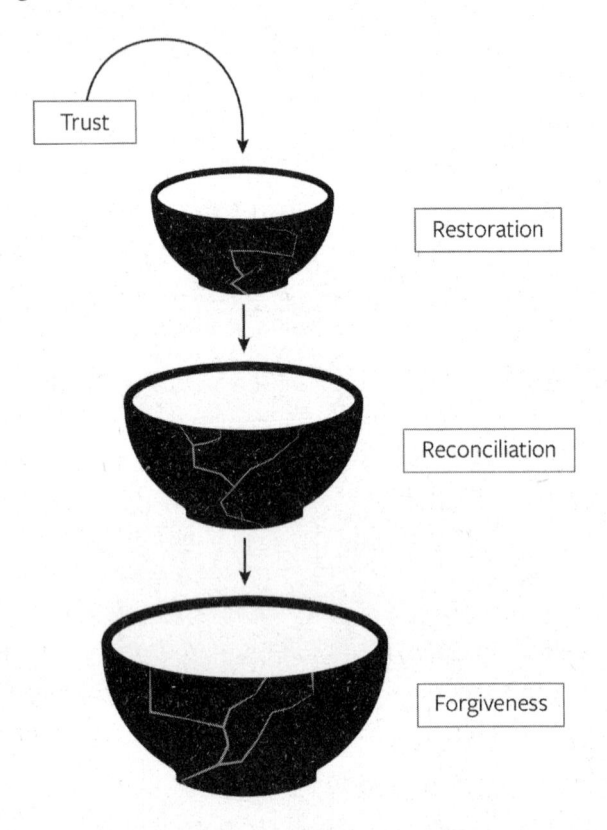

[Diagram: An arrow from a "Trust" label points down to three stacked bowls labeled, from top to bottom, "Restoration," "Reconciliation," and "Forgiveness."]

The Need for Restored Trust

If *forgiveness*, *reconciliation*, and *restoration* are like three bowls progressively nested into each other, then *trust* is like the healing water poured into them. Over time your husband must *deposit* trust drop by drop into your relationship, and you must *collect* it. This is a joint endeavor, but *he* must initiate it.

Let's expand our analogy to illustrate what I'm talking about. Like water, trust can be rather fluid. Its level ebbs based on the conditions of the surrounding environment and how consistently it's deposited. Initially it requires daily maintenance if it is to remain at a sufficient level. There may even be blistering-hot days that test trust or cause it to evaporate. Amid the stressful "heat" shortly after your husband's disclosure, you may feel a continual need for deposits of assurance from your husband that are expressed in visible actions. He may tire or even bristle under the weight of this need, which can make your journey through aftershock all the more difficult or confusing. Hopefully appropriate and realistic trust deposits are something the two of you can define and discuss one-on-one and in counseling.

The good news is that just as water can eventually saturate dry places and turn them into an oasis, growing trust creates a progressively more restful place in the relationship.

In a very real way, you've been traumatized, and everyone, yourself included, must be patient and understand the complex effects of trauma on your body, mind, and spirit. However, with care and planful responses to your trauma, you can begin to experience moments of relief and eventually even refreshment.

Restoring Trust Takes Time

Experiencing a stable sense of trust and consistent positive feelings in your relationship will take far more than a few weeks, and most often trust isn't *fully* realized until a number of years have passed. Randy and Marcia's story illustrates this important point:

Randy gave Marcia a sheepish look. Then he turned to the therapist and shrugged.

"I really don't know what to tell you," he said. "I said I was sorry, and I meant it. I've kept my promise, too. It's been nearly a month since I've looked at pornography. We've been coming to these sessions for three weeks now! How much longer is this going to take?"

The counselor looked him straight in the eye. "That depends on you," she said quietly. "It will take as long as it needs to take, and the more you pressure Marcia to trust you, the harder she'll find it to do. You have to try to see things from her perspective. Your damaging behavior has cut her to the core of her femininity. There's almost nothing you could do that would wound her more deeply. You've got to patiently and humbly follow a recovery plan that shows heart-level transformation and new, sincere relational skills, not merely a brief behavior change."

A new era of restored trust occurs when open, transparent, and accountable practices are a new normal in your marriage, and safe, intimate conversations occur on a regular basis. Living in *this* way is living out restoration with the "water" of trust consistently in your bowl.

Ways Your Husband Can Help Restore Your Trust in Him

"I'm trying to trust you, Will," Vicky said as they finished up the dinner dishes, "but it's really hard. I'm afraid of being hurt again."

"What am I doing that makes you still doubt me?" Will asked with a hint of frustration.

"Well, when I'm out of the house, I just hate that you might be on your computer on a pornography site again. I really do wish you would move your computer to the family room and actually put controls on your accessibility to pornography sites."

"You mean you want me to give up the only privacy I have at home and put my computer in the middle of our family life? How can I even play an innocent game without the kids running around and making it hard to think?"

"Yes, I do mean just that," Vicky answered.

Like Will, husbands who have broken their wives' trust may have to make uncomfortable adjustments until they can repair what has been broken. One way they can help themselves is to become part of a men's recovery group. Many of these groups assist husbands by providing a list of "best practices" that help them avoid overwhelming temptation during this period in their lives. They agree to abide by these specific practices and check in on a regular basis with their counselor and other supportive men in their group. If they have a slip or experience intense temptation, they discuss what it means and learn how to respond in a way that shows integrity. They can also learn to move through their toxic shame or tendency to hide in embarrassment. They learn new relational skills.

With your input, your husband may also list behaviors that are meaningful and represent a true trust deposit to your heart. For some wives, that might include a willing phone call or sending a selfie photo that proves their husbands' whereabouts after a timely arrival at a known destination. Or it might involve offering to downgrade technology and live with certain computer or phone inconveniences for a period of time, simply because marital trust is more valuable to the husband than convenience at this critical stage of recovery. Sharing passwords, deleting problematic social media accounts, cutting off or minimizing risky relationships, and changing jobs are all examples of important actions husbands must often take to help initially restore their wives' broken trust.

If Your Husband Yields to Temptation

You may have noticed that I used the word *slip* in the previous section. Unfortunately, your husband is engaged in an intense battle, so successfully quitting "cold turkey" all pornography use, masturbation, or habitual forms of acting out is unlikely, even though it's possible.

Even the thought of this possibility can strike panic, or even deep anger, in the already-burdened heart of a wife in your situation. That's why it may help to have general categories and terminology you can use should your husband act out in an inappropriate way in the future. Acknowledging and preparing for this possibility, however, is *not* a license for your husband to return to old ways. It's simply a wise safety precaution you can take that may offer *security* and some measure of *predictability* to both of you.

Think of it like keeping a fire extinguisher under your kitchen sink. You never aim to use it, but it's there if needed. With a contingency plan, each of you knows what to look for and what to do if another unhealthy choice or blatant sin occurs. Making a plan is not something to do all by yourselves. It would be impossible to predict the myriad circumstances or situations that might demand various responses. You must seek guidance from your counselor(s) that's specific to your story and personal histories.

What useful terminology can you draw upon if the need arises to dialogue with your spouse and counselor? Let's consider the words *slip*, *lapse*, and *relapse*. Employing such terminology with your spouse can prevent both of you from responding to a *slip* as if it's a full-blown *relapse*, and vice versa.[2]

- A *slip* is best understood as a brief failure in judgment that leads to an imperfection in recovery and a form of acting out that's challenging to eliminate without some learned skill, effort, or empowering insight.

- A bit farther down the path is what some would call a *lapse*. This is when a poor decision or slip has developed into something more willful but brief. Rationalization or skirting the full truth by telling half-truths (usually owing to recognizable toxic shame) may have occurred, but only initially. Your spouse crosses a line but then returns to his senses, owns up to his lapse in judgment (as hard as that admission may be), and recommits to the recovery plan. This prevents a full-blown relapse into the cycles of addiction and potentially redoubles commitment to healthier actions.

- When fully conceived and repeated, a lapse can become a *relapse*. During a relapse, your husband's behavior looks very much like what was occurring before he started the recovery process. He returns to a secret life of pornography use or other sexual infidelities, along with lies, deception, and cover-ups, which often continue until he is "caught" again.

Due to the various dangers a slip, lapse, or relapse pose to a man's recovery and a fragile marriage (especially in these early stages), I'll say once again that guidance is essential in forming a marital-response plan for each of these possibilities. Likewise, a man in recovery needs a well-defined safety plan to prevent further progression toward a relapse should he stumble or even willfully cross a line that goes against agreed-upon boundaries. Yes, natural consequences may vary, but open, honest confession and following a safety plan can demonstrate a continued commitment to personal recovery. Your heart and your marriage are important enough to place these kinds of safety nets underneath them. Despite the imperfect paths that some men take, a man's willingness to confess his shortcomings and diligently seek what can be gleaned from every sin and mistake is of paramount importance. This is exactly the process Larry followed.

Larry came home from work with a splitting headache. His schedule had been so busy lately, he hadn't paused for exercise or a truly healthy meal in several days. He crashed on the couch for what he thought might be a nap, but when he rolled over on the TV remote, memories of his typical way of "zoning out" and relaxing came to mind.

No one was home.

Maybe I'll flip a few channels to see what's there. It's just a way to relax, he thought.

His internal dialogue didn't match the principles he'd been recently exposed to in his recovery counseling. But not recognizing his vulnerability and desperately wanting to escape from discomfort, Larry took the "medicine" he'd taken hundreds, if not thousands, of times before.

He thought he'd just watch a racy show, but a few clicks of the remote was all it took to get him sucked into an available adult channel. He had done it again, and shortly after masturbating, he could hardly believe how quickly he had jumped back into that behavior after all that had happened over the past month. He panicked. He wanted to lie, but he also knew that his wife, his counselor, and his recovery group would soon be asking questions and talking about this slip.

Unlike anything he'd ever done before, he got up, called his primary accountability partner, and later journaled about the incident, the conditions leading up to it, his choices, and what he could do differently in the future.

As hard as it was, and as much as it hurt and stirred familiar flashbacks for his wife, Kim, he read the whole journal entry to her the next day. She was angry, of course, but Larry also knew he couldn't get better without honesty, nor could their marriage.

It took several counseling sessions after Larry's confession for Kim to even *begin* to trust him again. She could see that he had recognized his perilous situation before it had gotten any worse, but she couldn't believe he'd been so foolish as to go back to flipping channels and watching racy shows, which is how his numerous online hookups had started in the first place.

Larry said he learned the following lessons from his slip:

> I have to know how work stress and lack of physical self-care trigger me into a strong desire to "medicate" with pornography. I now know that if I even think about the TV remote and those channels, I need to run the other way. I've also got to call the cable company and change our package. And truth be told, part of me had probably conveniently "forgotten" to block those channels because I foolishly thought I could dabble around in sin without it being a full-blown issue.

The Counselor's Plan Is Key

Slips or a longer lapse in judgment that includes a lie followed by repentance feels especially maddening or crushing to the wife. A wife cannot and *should not* be her husband's "babysitter" or monitor, and especially not his primary or exclusive accountability partner. Yet she can't remain fully in the dark either.

A skilled counselor is the one to help you and your husband come up with a plan that includes various forms and frequency of communication about your husband's progress and the challenges he faces. Your husband will communicate with the counselor and supportive men in his life to stay accountable, and they'll need to keep you informed of his progress. Plans often include periodic check-ins with the recovery counselor, and a pastor and/or another stable, mature accountability partner. Your husband's forthright sharing at regular intervals and growing emotional intimacy with you are key. This is where the skills you both learned during intensive marital therapy will be especially useful.

Eventually the effort your husband invests in recovery can lead to greater safety and trust in your relationship based on what he's said and done consistently over time.

How You Respond to His Efforts

Once your husband begins to make such important and genuine efforts toward restoring trust, you can hopefully be ready to emotionally receive those trust deposits into your heart in a meaningful way.

Your job is to maintain goodwill in the journey and rightly evaluate and discern these deposits for what they are. It's not that you need to be lenient or an easy sell. Not at all. But you do need to fairly recognize what is occurring in your husband's life and acknowledge it if he is making true and sincere investments. Even if his record is imperfect, is he genuine and moving increasingly in the right direction? What is his overall trajectory, and what does he do if he slips or stumbles with an addictive tendency? Is he committed to his recovery plan or simply making things up based on his own authority?

By now you're probably able to view the overall situation and read whether your husband is sincere in his recovery efforts. If he is and you still have trouble even *trying* to trust him, something else may be going on within you.

If practicing self-care and maintaining spiritual and emotional health aren't occurring in your life, it will eventually seem to you and your husband that no matter how many trust deposits he makes, it will never make a difference. It's as if the three bowls just aren't able to fully hold the water despite both of your efforts. At that point, either of you is more likely to give up on positive change. Hearts can become sullen or hard.

This is understandable, of course. You've been through a lot. But what if there's more to your healing and needs than you realize? You and your marriage deserve the time and attention it takes to remove barriers to your peace and progress.

What Else Might Block Your Ability to Trust Your Husband?

Betrayal Trauma

Jenna was having a peaceful weekend morning—one of her first in months. The stress of the revelations of her husband Ryan's frequent pornography use had taken its toll for sure, but since he sincerely engaged counseling and his group, Jenna told herself that she had reasons for rest and hope. The night before, he'd even shown her his recovery journal, and one of his trusted recovery partners had been at their home for a cookout and prayer time.

During the afternoon, though, Jenna was folding laundry in their bedroom and felt increasingly flush and ill. Her heart was literally racing, and as she thought about the remainder of her task and day, she could hardly face them.

It was the fifteenth of the month. And interestingly, exactly six months ago on the fifteenth was when she shockingly found the first clear evidence of Ryan's behavior in their bedroom.

To add to her tumultuous afternoon, Ryan left for a quick twenty-minute trip to the grocery store. Near panic flooded Jenna in the moment she heard the garage door close upon his departure. She had no sense of safety, and she incessantly imagined scenarios about his short trip out that had hardly any plausible grounding in objective reality.

Jenna's experience is just one small sample of the effects trauma sets in place and the flashbacks that happen.

Like Jenna, the types of betrayal events you've been through likely represent significant trauma to your body, mind, and spirit. If this seems to describe you, then there are additional extensive "betrayal trauma" resources that you and your well-informed counselor can consider utilizing. Trauma-informed counseling and interventions can be very key, if not essential.

The inability to fittingly trust your husband or others in your life when reasonable evidence supports it is often a natural and protective instinct. It's the body's and the brain's way of creating a sense of safety.

However, this good survival mechanism can get "stuck" and remain active in a way that eventually inhibits desired progress.

Seeing the experience through a lens of trauma can be freeing. Your trauma responses aren't because you're extra "faulty" or broken. They're because you're normal and your mind is designed to stay safe. Oftentimes, wives need time and professional help to calibrate this survival mechanism and move through effects of the traumatic events.

Wounds of the Distant Past

Bethany grew up in a family that appeared to be the Christian ideal. Her parents volunteered weekly at their church. She and her two older brothers received good grades and never caused trouble. No one struggled with any serious problems, so everything seemed all right—at least on the outside.

Bethany learned at an early age, however, not to talk about conflicts that might be churning inside her heart or her home. Emotional needs were considered unimportant and generally ignored in her family. Her dad seemed to have plenty of time to give to church members and her brothers. But seldom did he show any interest in Bethany or extend love and affirmation to her.

Once she confided her feelings of rejection to her mother. In response, her mother shamed Bethany for not being appreciative.

One day Bethany drove home crying because her boyfriend had asked someone else to the homecoming dance. She didn't expect any support from her family, but she was unprepared for the jokes that were directed at her during dinner. Bethany's heart was broken—first by her boyfriend and then by her family. That night she vowed silently that she would never get hurt again.

Whether it's a hurt like Bethany's or something even more serious, such as a betrayal in an earlier marriage, rape or sexual abuse, or another deeply wounding event, that wound may never have healed. If it hasn't, you might have a severely limited capacity to acknowledge your husband's positive recovery efforts or receive his trust deposits now that he has added to that earlier wound.

The inability to even *imagine* trusting your husband again is one of the greatest threats to restoration. What seems impossible may never even be attempted or, if initially attempted, may quickly be abandoned at the first major challenge. Sadly, this form of short-circuiting trust and restoration happens all too frequently. It can easily fly under the radar because you've been focused on your husband's problem.

Your counselor is key, once again, in helping you discover any earlier wounds that have caused damage and work on healing them. Once you begin this work, you'll be in a much better place to receive your husband's sincere trust deposits, assuming he's on that trajectory in his recovery.

Back to the Three Bowls

Now that we've examined the issue of trust, let's return to the illustration of the three bowls that appears at the beginning of this chapter.

The bowl at the bottom of the diagram represents *forgiveness*.

The bowl in the middle represents *reconciliation*.

The bowl at the top represents *restoration*.

Remember that as these bowls progressively nest inside each other, they become a single unified stack. In the recovery process, *forgiveness* leads to *reconciliation*, and *reconciliation* leads to *restoration*.

Bowl 1: Forgiveness

Forgiveness is God's call and requirement of us as His followers. Colossians 3:13 says, "[Forgive] each other; as the Lord has forgiven you, so you also must forgive." This is an individual matter and isn't necessarily dependent on your husband's actions. Forgiveness is the largest "bowl" that holds the other two bowls and must be present for reconciliation and restoration to take place. However, forgiving doesn't mean you should be naive or let your husband take advantage of you. On the contrary, it's a matter of releasing yourself from bondage to the resentment and bitterness that may be holding you hostage.

Forgiveness is God's remedy for neutralizing destructive or seething anger by placing yourself, your husband, and your entire marriage completely in His hands. It means being obedient to

Scripture. It's God's invitation to secure and deepen your hand-in-hand walk with Him as a beloved and empowered daughter of the King. Forgiveness is *not*

- to be tritely rushed;
- to be "forced" or "demanded of you" by another human being;
- a way to simply bury emotions;
- immediately trusting the offender again;
- forgetting to keep out of harm's way;
- condoning or excusing the offense;
- minimizing or justifying the behavior;
- showing leniency or exonerating the offender from necessary restorative actions (e.g., going "soft" on the hard-but-redemptive recovery work required);
- balancing the scales (exacting revenge);
- using a ledger system to measure out the amount of grace you "owe" based on your own shortcomings by comparison;
- making a guilt payment to your spouse for the ways you've hurt him; or
- reconciling with your husband (agreeing on the record of events) or restoring your marriage (coming back together again), although these two steps *can* be desired and eventual *outcomes* of forgiveness.

There's also an important difference between the *choice* of forgiveness and the *emotion* of forgiveness. Once you've made up your mind to let go of your husband's past offenses and forgive him, it will take time for your feelings to catch up with your decision. Forgiveness is both a spiritual decision point you come to and a process that unfolds. The emotional changes don't necessarily happen overnight. You can't simply snap your fingers and put everything back the way it was *before* the cyber-affair or the pornography addiction began. You've not only been betrayed and deeply hurt, but you've actually had to learn to accept your pain as a way of life. It's going to take time to get beyond this aftershock phase in your life.

Ideally you'll eventually integrate this hurt into your life story with a sense of God's help and peace. Your life story now includes the betrayal of trust that happened in your marriage relationship. You no longer deny it, try to erase it from your memory, or live as if it never happened.

This is why the trite phrase "forgive and forget" is inaccurate and unhelpful. You can forgive without having to keep trying to forget.

True biblical forgiveness *means*

- giving up unhealthy anger, which is often revealed in bitterness, the silent treatment, or revenge;
- facing up to the true nature and personal impact of the offense and willingly dealing with the injury it has inflicted;
- turning over to God both the offense and the offender;
- choosing to release your own demand for justice in punishing the other person;

- if it's safe to do so, demonstrating a willingness to work with the wrongdoer to achieve deeper mutual understanding and empathy; and

- staying open to the possibility of a renewed relationship.

Forgiveness allows you to grasp that God has forgiven you and is redeeming your sin and shortcomings with His supernatural love. It also reveals your need for God's love so you can forgive others as well.

Bowl 2: Reconciliation

Unlike forgiveness, reconciliation is a *joint* venture. It means that you and your husband agree on what happened and are no longer in a battle over the facts and reality of where things stand.

Reconciliation doesn't necessarily mean restoration. Couples may agree on what happened and find a way to cope or make peace with it, only to return to separate corners in their lives. Oddly, coping may even include divorce or living virtually apart in the same home. Sadly, if one or both partners aren't willing to actively participate in the recovery process, protective distance might be necessary.

Occasionally, though, husbands or wives settle for a less-than-full recovery because they might not realize there's more healing to come, or they simply might not want to do the work. These couples haven't yet realized the deeper potential of restoration. Maybe one of them—it can be either party—lacks the vision, skills, ability, or assistance to get there. I hope, however, that *both* of you will experience something better and greater ahead—something redemptive that's in line with God's character. It's called *restoration*.

Bowl 3: Restoration

This part of the joint venture is *biblical* reconciliation in the *fullest* sense of the word. Restoration fulfills God's heart and purpose in a way that puts His redemptive characteristics and love on display. It means that you and your husband have progressively forgiven and reconciled and are now working on repairing and rebuilding your relationship and intimacy.

Restoration is the best relapse-prevention plan. Consider Jeremiah 33:6, when God revealed to Judah and Israel His plan for restoration: "Behold, I will bring to [this city] health and healing, and I will heal [My people] and reveal to them abundance of prosperity and security."

God's lavish nature and desire are to restore your marriage *beyond* any of the good things you experienced before—blessing you with more relational vision, health, and enjoyment. At the end of this journey, you may even find yourselves enjoying your marriage in a deeper way for the first time ever!

Powerful Potential to Achieve Forgiveness, Reconciliation, and Restoration

Perhaps what these nesting bowls represent seems far out of reach to you right now. Remember, the power of God is working in and through your life to bring about His will for you. He's recorded times in the past when He has restored above and beyond what was lost:

AFTERSHOCK

As for you also, because of the blood of my covenant
    with you,
  I will set your prisoners free from the waterless pit.
Return to your stronghold, O prisoners of hope;
  today I declare that I will restore to you double.

ZECHARIAH 9:11-12

Instead of your shame there shall be a double portion;
  instead of dishonor they shall rejoice in their lot;
therefore in their land they shall possess a double
    portion;
  they shall have everlasting joy.

ISAIAH 61:7

The Lord restored the fortunes of Job, when he had prayed for his friends. And the Lord gave Job twice as much as he had before.

JOB 42:10

After you have suffered a little while, the God of all grace, who has called you to his eternal glory in Christ, will himself restore, confirm, strengthen, and establish you.

1 PETER 5:10

As for you, you meant evil against me, but God meant it for good, to bring it about that many people should be kept alive, as they are today.

GENESIS 50:20

Helping Children Understand What's Going On

If you have children, they're also going to need some help working their way through this family crisis. Older children may already know what's been happening; younger kids will have sensed stress in the home and will need someone to come alongside them as they deal with feelings they don't really understand.

Your counselor could refer you to another counselor who specializes in helping children. Or you may have a friend, youth pastor, or family member your children feel especially close to who could spend time with them and talk through what is happening in their family. Maybe an aunt or uncle or grandparent could take each child out separately for lunch or a milkshake, talk with that child in a nonthreatening environment, and be a loving presence.

It's especially important to assure children of all ages that they're emotionally and physically safe, and you won't allow anything to harm them or threaten their security.

I'd advise you to resist the temptation to pretend that nothing is going on or keep your children totally in the dark concerning this serious issue in your marriage. Some parents might try to hush up the whole thing. Others may feel a need to lie about the counseling sessions they're attending. That's not a good idea. Honesty is always the best policy—allowing, of course, for age-appropriate language and content. Whatever you do, handle the topic sensitively and don't overload your children with unnecessary details.

Depending on your children's ages, you can use broad conversation starters, such as "Mom and Dad are getting help for our relationship," or "We love each other, and sometimes disappointments and problems happen that God helps us solve through counseling. That's what we're doing because our family is so important to us. We want you to know where we're going, but we don't want you to worry. Do you have any questions?"

Follow your children's lead. Don't give them more information than they're asking for, but don't withhold or lie. These are tender and teachable moments, and your children need your reassurance while you're devoting a lot of necessary attention to yourself and your marriage. If you have close friends, babysitters, or extended family whom your children especially enjoy and feel comfortable with, this is a time to enlist their help so your children are well cared for while you and your husband spend time in personal reflection, conversations, or counseling sessions.

Continuing Your Journey

You clearly have a lot on your plate right now. Exercising your faith in God will help you feel His companionship day by day through the aftershock and initial recovery from your husband's destructive behaviors. You don't have to try to figure everything out today.

Though you may have only recently discovered the painful reality that your marriage is in trouble, the truth is that the situation has taken months and years to get to this point. As a result, it will take time to bring about forgiveness, reconciliation, and restoration. Regardless of what your spouse decides to do, *you* can choose to live fully and receive the peace and joy

God offers along the way. You can also choose to forgive your husband the way we discussed in this chapter.

God is faithful, and He will never let you down or stop loving you!

REFLECTION
> When I am afraid,
>> I put my trust in you.
>
> PSALM 56:3

QUESTIONS
1. This is a power-packed chapter that contains some hard and maybe even unexpected messages. Which concepts or stories had the greatest impact on you? Journal about one or two of them. What invitation is God holding out to you that is consistent with His character?

2. What emotions are you feeling after reading this chapter? Think about them and write down your thoughts and feelings in your journal.

3. Reread the section "Powerful Potential to Achieve Forgiveness, Reconciliation, and Restoration" and review the Bible verses in context. What are your thoughts as you consider this section? Write about them in your journal.

PRAYER
Dear Lord, I can't regain trust in my husband without Your help. I shouldn't trust until there's sound reason to do so—but I can trust You. Help me know how, when, and what to trust in

my relationship with my husband. I'm also a human being who stumbles in many ways. Help me show humility and take firm, balanced actions that will call my husband out of sin and into recovery. May I also exercise responsibility for myself in these areas and have your compassionate help to realize and process my own trauma. On this road to recovery, help each of us cooperate with Your abundant ability to restore.

CHAPTER 9
YOUR SEXUAL RELATIONSHIP WITH YOUR HUSBAND

A man shall leave his father and his mother and hold fast to his wife, and they shall become one flesh.

GENESIS 2:24

ROBIN HAD AN INDIVIDUAL APPOINTMENT with me after I'd been seeing her and her husband, Mike, for several weeks. She tearfully explained a problem she was struggling with:

> Since Mike repented of his pornography use and we've been meeting with you, he's been asking me to begin having sex with him again.
> We haven't had sex since I discovered his behavior, and he has assumed that our process of intensive counseling would mean that I'd be willing, and even excited, to be intimate with him again.
> I'm not.

I do feel a bit guilty because he is doing all you've suggested. I also tell him I do love him, and he says he finds that confusing, since I still won't resume sexual relations. I don't know exactly why I feel this way, but I just do.

Is it okay *not* to want to have sex with my husband?

An Important Question

Robin asked an important question that many other women have asked me. My answer may apply to you, too.

For the time being, yes, it's okay not to want to have sex with your husband. Such feelings are normal and understandable. They're to be expected for a woman whose spouse has violated the marriage through his involvement with pornography, cybersex, or complete physical adultery. Also, do you recall the things mentioned in the previous chapter about betrayal trauma and other barriers to trust? These each play a part in your sexual interest and response too.

However, on the opposite side of the coin, it's okay too if you do desire sex with your spouse. (A variety of responses can occur because our emotions and sexuality are complexly intertwined.) The main caution here (besides assuring that STD testing has occurred if necessary) is that neither spouse assumes that merely having "lots of sex" somehow solves the problem.

Point is, as we've already seen, an offense like this isn't just a minor scratch on the surface of a marriage. It's a deep and painful breach of trust that goes straight to the heart of the marital relationship.

Even if you've made a *rational* decision to forgive your husband, it will probably take some time for your heart to catch up with your head. Your husband's repentance and faithful behavior may aid the healing of that deep wound, but neither you nor your husband can force the rate of progress to speed up. Sexuality and intimacy are all about vulnerability, and you can't make yourself readily vulnerable again until you've gained real assurances that it's safe to do so. You could encourage your husband by letting him know that you're working on the sexual healing you need, and you appreciate his patience with you now.

You may have heard of a widely believed teaching that a man *has to* have sex at least every three days. And if his wife doesn't attend to his needs, he will virtually be forced to turn to pornography, prostitutes, online sex, or masturbation. This idea is not only a myth; it's an insult to both men *and* women. If your husband's repentance is real, and he's working on his recovery plan, he knows it's his responsibility to set boundaries that will help him stay away from his old behaviors. Fighting temptation won't be easy, but he can succeed. The choices he makes are his, and you are *not* responsible for what he does or doesn't choose.

Being pro-sex (nonprudish) and open to biblical sexuality in marriage doesn't mean you are a *slave* to every whim or instance of sexual desire that you or your spouse may have. Christopher West, a lecturer on theology and human sexuality, has observed that ". . . if we can't say no to our desires, our yes means nothing. If we can't say no, we're not free, and if we're not free, we're not able to love."[1]

The beautiful point here is, sex is meant to be *loving* and guided by the ever-growing fruit of the Spirit in our lives. It's meant to be *passionate*, and even *regular* within a marriage. Yet, for the act to be conditioned as compulsory and without freedom, I would have to agree with Christopher West's conclusion: "Sex in such a situation is merely akin to what animals do when they're in heat."[2]

The Benefits of a Sexual Hiatus

Millie and Gene had a slightly different struggle with the issue of resuming sexual relations than Robin and Mike did. But the solution is somewhat similar. Both Millie and Gene *wanted* to engage in sexual intimacy again. They were both in intensive counseling and felt that their healing was progressing. But something seemed off.

"We've tried taking a few days away from home to be in a new setting and enjoy being together," Gene told me, "but our sexual times still seem strained. I know it will take a while to restore our comfort with each other, but right now it seems stressful to keep trying."

Gene was describing a situation that might be improved by agreeing to a sexual hiatus. A sexual time-out might be a way of turning down the pressure created by unmet expectations.

When you do resume sex after a break, it can grow into something more inspired and wholly meaningful rather than perfunctory. Additional benefits also can be derived from a sexual hiatus:

1. Redistribution of power and responsibility. Human sexuality has its own power of expression. But like any form of power, it can be abused. A husband or wife can become demanding or wield power through strict refusals. Areas of responsibility can also become blurred.

2. Space to reevaluate the relationship and take responsibility for any abuses of power or distortions of *pure* desire by the contaminants in pornography.

3. Healing of the past and starting again.

4. An opportunity to reinstate sexual honesty, caring, and pure expressions through sex.

5. Grounding of the marriage in mutual commitment and fidelity.

6. Time to evaluate specific sexual activity. This is an ideal time to ponder what has been enjoyable as well as problematic in the lovemaking experience.

7. Neurological detoxification. In chapter 5, we talked about the biochemical aspects of sexual addiction. The pornography addict needs a sexual time-out to detoxify his brain's heightened sexual chemistry. It's believed that this biochemical rebalancing can be significantly kick-started through thirty days of intentional abstinence, which includes refraining from fantasizing and masturbation.

8. Discovery of emotions. Once the self-medicating anesthesia of sexual indulgence wears off, the pornography addict has a chance to thaw out emotionally. This in turn allows him to become better informed and more insightful about his own emotions.

9. An opportunity to practice the discipline of self-control. Abstinence from *any* powerful craving enhances self-control, which in turn gives the addict a greater sense of personal wellness. In this way, his distorted belief

that sex is his greatest need can be exposed as a lie and replaced with truth. Abstinence builds a foundation for the refreshing and God-intended practice of coordinating with, and at times waiting for, his bride.

The Necessity of Mutual Consent

Dale and Frannie had reconnected sexually after Dale's repentance and sincere efforts to restore their marriage. Frannie was also meeting with her counselor, and Dale and Frannie seemed to be establishing a pleasant new normal.

Dale had always wanted Frannie to engage in some sexual activities she found undesirable. The activities didn't involve pornography, but they were outside Frannie's comfort zone. As a loving wife trying to restore her marriage, she wondered, *Should I agree to engage in activities I find highly undesirable or even offensive?*

The answer to Frannie's question is "Absolutely not!"

As part of the healing process, there will certainly come a time when you will want to resume normal sexual relations with your husband, as well as grow into your sexual future. But at *no* point is there any reason to subject yourself to sexual activities that violate your wishes or disregard your comfort level.

If your husband demands this of you, you'll likely need to take another respectful break from sex and talk through your differences as you seek to reengage in this important part of your marriage.

During the course of those discussions, your husband will hopefully be growing and embracing the truth that marital sex is about love, and that love requires each spouse to treat the needs, feelings, desires, and preferences of his or her mate as matters of the highest priority. If something is a big deal to one partner, it's a big deal to both.

Mutual consent is basic to all healthy sexual expression in marriage. *Consent* implies that both parties know what's proposed and expected; that they fully understand the physical and emotional ramifications of the suggested activity; that there is room for discussion; and that both partners are always free to say a simple no, or anything along this spectrum, including *"Not now," "I would like to take time to consider my feelings about it,"* or *"I don't think I'll ever be open to that specific activity."*

Respect, humility, and forbearance, which are essential to all healthy human relationships, are each of great importance for you both.

Get Rid of Lingering Misinformation

Savannah came to see me soon after she was divorced. My compassion and sadness for her were amplified because the end of her marriage was one more statistic, and although the people trying to help didn't cause the breakup, they certainly added more fuel to the pain.

When Savannah and Anthony had been married only about six months, she found out that he was severely addicted to pornography. It was a devastating discovery. Savannah now felt that everything her new husband had told her while they were dating had been a lie. She came to the conclusion that he had married her mainly in the belief that she could become the catalyst to help him break his pornography habit. There was no other way to make sense of his insistent demands for more and more aggressive and then deviant sex.

Realizing that Anthony's problem was only getting worse, Savannah reached out for help. She talked to some Christian friends and later to her pastor. Oddly enough, they all told her the same thing: "Men are simply wired to want more sex than women. In fact, they have to have a sexual release at least every seventy-two hours to stay on an even keel. A wise and submissive wife understands this and gives her husband what he wants. It's the only way he can avoid and conquer temptations."

Savannah took their word for it, but somehow her feelings of discomfort only increased. She was desperate to find a way to feel okay about what Anthony was doing. It didn't work. Meanwhile, all of her personal wants, needs, and desires as a wife went suppressed or unfulfilled. Sex with her husband was only a mechanical act. On some occasions Savannah felt that she was "his pornography."

The turning point came when she arrived home early one day and found him watching a movie far more perverse than anything she could have imagined. For Savannah, it was the last straw. Their marriage quickly fell apart. The couple was divorced before the year was out.

Thousands if not millions of women around the globe could echo Savannah's story. Everywhere there are men using or addicted to sexually illicit material who think that marriage and a willing wife can somehow fix their problem. Everywhere there are women—many of them dutiful Christian wives—who have been led to believe that it's *their* responsibility to pull their husbands out of this dark abyss by catering to their every sexual whim. Everywhere voices are telling women that they can't be "good" wives unless they're constantly "available" to their husbands, no matter the cost to their personal integrity.

Men, say some professional sources, are sexual animals who can't help the way they are. Women simply have to learn how to live with the implications. It's a vicious cycle, and it condemns these wives to an overresponsible and unfulfilling sexual duty. These well-meaning perspectives, which claim to be based on the view that this script for male and female sexuality was crafted by God, are veritable sexual heresies. They make confused wives like Savannah feel trapped in their marriages, and they misrepresent healthy, godly sexuality as it's intended. God's design for sexual intimacy was an amazing gift from the beginning that we're invited to discover and explore in marriage with mutual consent and joint consideration.

God's Mysterious and Beautiful Design for Sexual Relationships

Sexual sin violates God's divine, fulfilling, faithful, and safe design for human sexuality in marriage. That violation creates deep wounds that hinder our ability to experience sex inside marriage the way God wants us to.

Genesis 2:24 says, "A man shall leave his father and his mother and hold fast to his wife, and they shall become one flesh." But all too often we let these words roll off our tongues without giving any serious thought to the mystery and symbolism of sex as it's described in the Bible, or how it's designed to contribute to human happiness and wholeness.

My friend Natalie told me about a glimpse she had of how that "one flesh" union is supposed to unfold:

> I was sitting in the church before the wedding
> ceremony started for the daughter of a good friend.
> The organ music was floating softly over the guests as

the pews began to fill up with friends and family of the bride and groom.

June, my friend's daughter, had been dating Hank for about two years as they both finished college. I knew that both sets of parents were delighted with these young people's choices of a life partner.

Both the bride and groom came from Christian families and wanted to base their marriage and their lives together on the design God originally intended. They had kept their commitment to abstain from sex until after marriage and were now about to experience that union.

After the grandparents and parents of the bride and groom were seated, the organ began the familiar strains of the wedding march, and June came down the aisle on the arm of her father.

I watched her glowing face as she fixed her eyes on Hank, who was waiting for her at the front of the church.

Then I looked at Hank. If June was glowing, Hank was absolutely beaming. The look on his face as he beheld his bride said it all. As they exchanged their vows, his anticipation of their union was evident in every movement—trembling hands, the slight shuffle of his feet, the grin that spread across his face, and the look in his eyes of cherishing this soul mate God had brought to him.

Lust was not what I saw. Nervousness was not what I saw. I saw love. It was obvious he was excited about what was about to happen, but there was so much more as both of them clasped hands and committed their lives to each other.

The mystery of it defies words, but the evidence of a sacred union declared the glory of God.

This couple is still together. I'm sure they have their share of marital ups and downs, but I also know that they began their marriage as God intended. Sexual intimacy was designed to be lived out in the context of marriage. It's the positive *ideal* or *prototype* of the marriage relationship.

Please understand that I'm *not* sharing this to make you feel guilty about how your marriage may have begun or how it has fallen short of the "standard." *Every* marriage falls short. We are *all* imperfect sinners. We are all sexually broken in some way and aspect because our sexuality is so closely intertwined with our humanness. June and Hank won't have a perfect marriage either. But they honored and pleased God by choosing His plan for the beginning of their life together.

It's normal to have ups and downs in the marital sexual journey. Sex is created for a lifetime of growth in a marriage. It's unifying. It's difficult at times. And it's sacred.

I'm always surprised that Christians and non-Christians alike seem to think that God isn't interested in our sex lives, or that if He *is* interested, His main goal is to take away our fun by subjecting us to a lot of unrealistic, constraining, maybe even mean-spirited rules.

I strongly disagree with thinking of God as a cosmic killjoy. After all, Genesis 1:28 says, "God blessed [the man and woman]. And God said to them, "Be fruitful and multiply and fill the earth and subdue it."

Think of that! Before any other command, before humanity's fall into sin, before human history had even begun, the Lord's first word to His children was "Go have sex!" And He made sure that this exhortation was recorded in His Holy Word so that all future generations would know about it.

But that's not all. The Bible is filled from beginning to end with passages that underscore this idea. One of my favorites is Proverbs 30:19 (emphasis added), where the writer pondered four deep mysteries too wonderful for the human mind to comprehend:

> The way of an eagle in the sky,
>   the way of a serpent on a rock,
> the way of a ship on the high seas,
>   *and the way of a man with a virgin.*

The Song of Solomon is a poetic celebration of this same mystery. Its theme from beginning to end is romantic love and sexual bonding between husband and wife. In the past, this book was often interpreted strictly as a story about God's relationship with His chosen people, but there's more to it than this. It's also a profound and intensely *sensual* study of the interaction between a man and a woman within the bond of matrimony.

The Old Testament prophets consistently used marriage and marital sex as illustrations of Israel's relationship with Yahweh. The apostle Paul followed in this same tradition when he quoted an Old Testament verse from Genesis 2 and then compared it to the relationship between Christ and the church: "'Therefore a man shall leave his father and mother and hold fast to his wife, and the two shall become one flesh.' This mystery is profound, and I am saying that it refers to Christ and the church" (Ephesians 5:31-32).

Then there's that powerful passage 1 Corinthians 6:16-18. I love the way Eugene Peterson paraphrases it in *The Message*:

> There's more to sex than mere skin on skin. Sex is as much spiritual mystery as physical fact. As written in Scripture, "The two become one." . . . We must not pursue the kind of sex that avoids commitment and intimacy, leaving us more lonely than ever—the kind of sex that can never "become one." There is a sense in which sexual sins are different from all others. In sexual sin we violate the sacredness of our own bodies, these bodies that were made for God-given and God-modeled love, for "becoming one" with another.

This thread of scriptural revelation reaches its peak in the final book of the Bible. In Revelation 19:9, sacred history finds its consummation in "the marriage supper of the Lamb." And in Revelation 21:2, we find the "new Jerusalem" described as a "holy city . . . coming down out of heaven from God, prepared as a bride adorned for her husband."

I think we can safely conclude that from the first page to the last, Scripture represents sex as a matter of the highest importance to God. It's a physical thing with a very intentionally designed heavenly meaning, and we're its stewards.

Sacred Sex

I remember speaking on this topic at a Christian physicians conference. I began by explaining that marital sex is good and a God-blessed, sacred spiritual act. I said that God wants a couple to build a foundation for their relationship by connecting deeply on mental, emotional, and spiritual levels. This leads to marriage. Only then, as a natural result or by-product of this profound soul connection, does it become appropriate for them to bond in sexual intercourse. This ever-deepening foundation of holistic human connection (not just body connection) is the context for meaningful marital sex. At this point my audience was smiling and nodding in agreement. That's when I asked some very personal questions and went over the scriptural evidence we had just reviewed.

"If you believe all of this evidence is true," I said, "then ask yourselves these questions: When was the last time you were making love and became aware that you were engaged in a spiritual act? Have you ever felt worshipful or sensitive to God's presence while you were having sex?"

The room fell deadly silent. The eyes of the people in the audience glazed over. So I asked, "What just happened here? Weren't we all in agreement that God created us as sexual beings—that He not only approves of but smiles down on and blesses the marital sex act?

"If you've never felt God's smiling presence during that union or considered the biblical symbolism bound up in your sexuality, what do you think that means?"

This is a good question. There's something amiss here, and we need to figure out why. When one or both partners in a marriage have been sexually wounded, whether through childhood abuse, rape, pornography, media distortions, promiscuity, or marital abuse, they frequently find it extremely difficult to think of sex as sacred.

I would add that the sexual heresies fed to Savannah and so many other Christians about how so-called "God-authored" sexual dynamics inevitably work between men and women also play a limiting and damaging role in our ability to view sex as sacred. As a result, many couples simply can't believe that the words *sex* and *spirituality* belong together in the same sentence.

The wonder of marital sex as it was meant to function in God's original plan is bigger, more breathtaking, and more all-encompassing in God's love story (the gospel) than most of us can imagine.

A New Mind-Set about Sexual Expression

This pure vision of sexuality is what God designed sex and marriage to look like when He made humankind in the beginning and pronounced all of His works *good*. But like everything else in God's good creation, the beauty and holiness of the sexual bond have been twisted, distorted, and compromised by human sin. Pornography and sexual addiction are a huge part of that destructive process.

Remember, marital sex is meant to be experienced within the wholeness of a person-to-person *relationship*. It's supposed to be based on intimacy, tenderness, mutual consent, and interpersonal sharing. As we've seen, it's about becoming *one flesh* with your spouse. This is why C. S. Lewis observed, "The monstrosity of sexual intercourse outside marriage is that those who indulge in it are trying to isolate one kind of union (the sexual) from all the other kinds of union which were intended to go along with it and make up the total union."[3]

In our current culture we certainly don't hear "sexual intercourse outside marriage" called a "monstrosity" very often. Even in the Christian community, a number of single adults now choose to live together outside the bond of marriage. Many a married Christian man (or woman) minimizes his sexual behavior and tries to excuse it instead of holding an image of a sacred union with his wife as the desire of his heart. Wives, too, often think of sex as a carnal act instead of an awesome gift from God.

Many couples can't even imagine what a godly sexual union would look like. It's a marvel and a reality that defies description. A good place to start is simply to think about what sacred sex could be as part of your marriage.

Consider how the various emotions of marriage and the physical actions shared between the male and female body show signs of God's nature or tell a symbolic story about it. He is a God of shared relationship and deep intimacy (the Trinity). He is faithful. He initiates and pursues us—and at our ready invitation, He then enters our lives and enables us to bear godly fruit. He is expressively passionate about His "marriage" covenant with His church, which the Bible refers to as the very bride of Christ. When our eyes are opened to the Creator's artwork in our bodies and in marital sexuality, we see obvious intentionality and many unfolding levels of beauty to be celebrated and enjoyed. In a very parallel way, God wants to "marry" each one of us so that we bear his name and the good results (the fruit) of our closeness with Him. Can you see the picture? Our commitment with God is like a *wedding*. Our closeness with Him is intimate like the *marriage bed*. The result is *life*—the human family that grows as a result of unity, sacrifice, and erotic love. Sex and our bodies, as God intended them, tell part of the gospel story.

Barbara and Kyle had been working on reconciling and restoring their marriage for about a year when they made a significant choice to change their thinking. Barbara told me about it one day in our counseling session:

> We had reengaged in a sexual relationship with each other but realized that the way we thought about sex wasn't the way we thought about anything else. In all other aspects of our lives, we had worked hard to study God's perspective and discern what His will and purpose were for whatever choices we made.
>
> But when it came to sex, we just had it as if it were another mundane thing we did together, like unloading the dishwasher. It was no longer tainted by Kyle's previous damaging behavior, but it wasn't a place where we invited God into our union.
>
> It took us a while to even think about God looking on us and blessing us. We had completely compartmentalized our sexual lives from our relationship with God. We were kind of embarrassed to talk about how to experience sacred sex. So we decided to just say a prayer asking God to be present with us, to touch our hearts, to clear our minds of unclean thoughts, and bless our union.
>
> I can't say that either of us ever saw a glowing aura or heard a celestial choir singing, but I can say that our sexual relationship changed for the better. It was much more about attitudes and nonverbal communication than about the sex act itself. It's a mystery for which we are grateful.

We also began to be much more communicative and faithful to invest in our sex life. This was because it now actually meant something more than a positive physical release. It was even tied to a deeper reality about our faith.

REFLECTION

"A man shall leave his father and mother and hold fast to his wife, and the two shall become one flesh." This mystery is profound, and I am saying that it refers to Christ and the church.

EPHESIANS 5:31-32

QUESTIONS

1. What are you most concerned about right now in your sexual relationship with your husband?

2. What do you think a sacred sex experience would feel and look like? What would you want to experience deep in your heart? Try to describe this in your journal.

PRAYER

God of my body, my mind, and my spirit, You made *all* of me and *all* of my husband—including our sexuality. My hope of having a pure or sacred sexual relationship seems far off or impossible. Would You patiently heal and *reinvigorate* us for *pure* intimacy that models You and Your nature? In time, help us share sex differently and more fully than we ever experienced before this recovery. Thank You for being patient with me and helping me learn patience as well. Give us Your vision. Amen.

CHAPTER 10

SETTING YOURSELF UP FOR SUCCESS

May the God of hope fill you with all joy and peace in believing, so that by the power of the Holy Spirit you may abound in hope.

ROMANS 15:13

I'VE WRITTEN THIS FINAL CHAPTER with the assumption that you and your husband are both working toward restoring your marriage. I deeply hope that you're moving forward together, but if not, please read on and realize that God loves you and has many blessings to bring into your life.

If you're alone in this endeavor, you'll benefit from modifying the spiritual vision, suggestions, and self-care tips in this chapter to yourself as a single individual or a married woman whose husband isn't joining her on this journey . . . yet.

I'd like to start with a hopeful and inspiring anecdote drawn from my files as a professional counselor. I pray that it will fuel the flames of your hope and desire for renewing healthy, redemptive, and supportive relationships.

Gene and Carol: A Success Story

Gene was an associate pastor at a midsize urban church with a strong and growing ministry. The whole congregation loved him. He was outgoing, interested in people, and willing to work hard to promote the gospel and God's Kingdom in the surrounding neighborhood. According to the senior pastor, Simon, Gene had done more to strengthen the church's outreach than any other associate he'd ever worked with. Furthermore, Simon considered Gene not only his closest friend, closer than a brother, but also a man of mature Christian faith.

Imagine Simon's shock when a woman from the congregation came to him with a disturbing secret. She had caught Gene viewing pornography on a church computer. She was discreet in her description of the incident, but Simon could tell that it had shaken her to her core. He immediately called Gene to his office.

"Yes," said Gene when he entered the room looking pale and distraught. The woman's accusation was true. What's more, this wasn't the first time he'd engaged in sexually inappropriate behaviors. Apparently, something similar had happened in two previous churches.

Hearing this, Simon probed Gene with a few questions about his background. Did he have a long history of sexually immoral behavior? Had he been promiscuous as a teen?

"No," said Gene.

"What about pornography?" asked Simon. "Have you had a long history with viewing pornography?"

Gene minimized it at first. But as the dialogue continued and Simon gently and persistently asked the question again and again, Gene finally broke down and conceded the full truth.

"I've been struggling with severe pornography issues for years," he admitted with tears in his eyes.

After ensuring that the female congregant was receiving the important care she needed to deal with her pain and shock, Simon asked to meet with Gene and his wife, Carol. He knew how common pornography addiction had become among men in the church, and he was no rookie when it came to supporting couples facing that marital crisis. He was, however, fully unprepared when Carol admitted she not only knew of Gene's pornography addiction but also that two previous churches had told Gene to either leave quietly or he'd be fired because of his problem.

Pastor Simon was dumbfounded. Years earlier, as chairman of the pulpit committee, he specifically asked each potential associate-pastor candidate if there was any moral failure in the man's past. Gene absolutely denied any past or current sexual sin.

Before offering Gene the leadership position, Simon met privately with Carol. She seemed equally as impressive as her husband. Simon even boldly asked her if Gene had any chronic sin patterns that needed to be addressed. She adamantly proclaimed, "No. We have a wonderful marriage, and you have nothing to worry about."

Pastor Simon had been masterfully deceived. How could his beloved ministry partner, Gene, have kept such a troubling secret from him and their faithful church members! How could Carol so skillfully lie for her husband!

"Gene promised me each time we moved to a new city that he was leaving his past behind," Carol told him. "I truly believed this time he would keep his promise, but nothing has changed. I just feel like giving up."

This was a moment of crisis. At that point anything could have happened. It might have meant the destruction of a marriage and family, as well as the end of a vital ministry. But for Gene and Carol, the senior pastor's wise handling of the situation made all the difference in the world.

His first step was to ask Gene for his resignation.

"This is a serious offense," he said. "Trust has been violated, and for the integrity and protection of our congregation, this has to be the outcome for your leadership role."

But he didn't leave the matter there. "I don't believe in shooting our wounded," he explained, "nor am I willing to shove you out into the cold without any kind of support. If you will commit to getting treatment, I'll commit to doing everything I can to get the two of you into counseling. And I want to meet with you here in my office for prayer and accountability once a week."

Next, Simon arranged an evening meeting with Gene, Carol, and all of the adults in the church. He started the session with a short message based on Romans 3:23: "For all have sinned and fall short of the glory of God." Then he gave the offender an opportunity to read a prepared statement. There wasn't a dry eye in the place as Gene made an open confession of his sins and his offense to his wife and others, including personal ownership of his wrongdoing.

When Gene had finished, Simon stood up again. "So where do we go from here, folks?" he said. "We could ostracize him, of course. Gene and Carol could just quietly disappear. The rest of the community wouldn't have to know why. It would be our little secret, and we could get the whole thing fixed without skipping a beat. Anybody want to second that motion?"

No one responded. You could have heard a pin drop.

"Well, then," said the pastor after a pause, "let me tell you what *I* think we ought to do. I've prayed and prayed about this, and I believe God is saying that He wants us to keep Gene and Carol as part of our fellowship to be restored. Naturally, Gene will no longer serve as a member of the staff, but he will be one of us in every sense of the term. The rest of us will make a commitment to attend to Gene's and Carol's needs. We'll see that Gene gets well-informed professional counseling. We'll hold his feet to the fire. We'll support Carol and love on both of them in every way we can.

"I also believe others of you here this evening may have similar sins to face. We're told to confess our sins and pray for each other. James 5:16 says, 'The prayer of a righteous person has great power.' We'll examine our own lives and make an effort to be honest with one another about our own sins. God not only wants to heal Gene and Carol and their marriage, but He also wants to heal our church. What do you think about that?"

The decision was unanimous. The congregation surrounded the couple with love and support. Boundaries and expectations were put in place, and they offered to help them cover the cost of intensive therapy with a competent Christian clinician. More than that, they agreed to organize a men's recovery and accountability group. Gene and Carol learned the importance of completing the assignments their counselor gave them, as well as continuing with follow-up therapy. Carol's friends from her Bible study group helped her not lose heart when she felt like giving up. As for the senior pastor, Simon became Gene's personal mentor.

The church gave Gene severance pay and stood by him until

he was able to find gainful employment. He and Carol continued as members of the congregation, and as a result of their example, two other men struggling with sexual compulsions found the courage to confess to their wives and then come forward to ask for help.

Gene and Carol made significant progress, and their marriage actually, although slowly, experienced forgiveness, reconciliation, and restoration. Carol's face glowed as she described the day they renewed their vows. Due to their choices and investments, God richly blessed and restored their marriage.

Sound too good to be true? Maybe so, but I can assure you that this couple's story is true. Only the names and some other details have been changed to maintain confidentiality. How do I know? Because I was Gene and Carol's therapist.

Arm for Spiritual Battle and Attend to Leftover Trauma

Ephesians 6:10-12 encourages us to "be strong in the Lord and in the strength of his might. Put on the whole armor of God, that you may be able to stand against the schemes of the devil. For we do not wrestle against flesh and blood, but against the rulers, against the authorities, against the cosmic powers over this present darkness, against the spiritual forces of evil in the heavenly places."

Few marital problems are as devastating as physical infidelity, and to be clear, other sexual sins of the mind or emotions that fall just short of physical contact can activate similar senses of damage. Sexual sins of this order don't simply break marital trust. They shatter it. For a believer, this kind of pain can even translate into a crisis of *faith* in the broadest sense. At the very least, the presence of serious sexual sin certainly causes trauma to the soul. These feelings and their effects on your faith and day-to-day actions are important to account for as you aim to heal.

As you grow spiritually, your *very growth* becomes a target of the evil one. Your and your husband's work together is a living, visible example of the power of the Holy Spirit and the mercy and love of God. So don't be surprised if the enemy targets your mind and you go back to pondering things you may previously have settled.

You might also feel an inordinate sense of suspicion toward your spouse. Maybe you've begun building credible trust, and your husband's actions show positive gains that ignite hope; however, panic and plaguing doubts are preoccupying your mind. Your unseen enemy takes advantage and nibbles at your progress. Suddenly that creeping doubt becomes a full-fledged spiritual assault amid the flashbacks of trauma. (Refer again to the barriers to trust described in Chapter 8.)

If fear and suspicion take over, then you may begin to interpret even the mundane things of everyday life through the lens of your spouse's former betrayal. In fact, feelings of fear can be so compelling that many wives will vigilantly check in on their husbands multiple times throughout the day in an attempt to monitor their every move.

To someone who has been emotionally traumatized and is under spiritual attack, such behavior seems rational. It's an attempt to take charge of circumstances that seem wildly out of control. The trouble is, it doesn't strengthen you. It actually weakens you. Tracking your spouse's every movement will only keep you trapped in a cycle of fear and suspicion. And your suspicions might not be true. Your husband may be living up to his promises.

That's not to say that you should give him carte blanche for the future or dismiss his need for healthy accountability. Real healing and reconciliation can't occur unless the guilty party is ready to be open and aboveboard about all of his comings and goings and social interactions.

Of course, you may feel like the ground beneath you is beginning to shake again for reasons other than spiritual assaults from the enemy. Your past experience may cause you to leap to inaccurate conclusions. Your husband might be struggling with temptations, and you might be afraid he'll succumb to those temptations.

Still, no matter where you are in your healing process, it's important to recognize that an unseen spiritual battle rages around you, and the leftover trauma in your heart can get reactivated in the most inopportune ways. Stay close to the Lord and hang on to your most helpful resources. Stay in touch with your therapist, whom God can use to help you address any trauma flashbacks. Relying on the Holy Spirit and engaging in good Christian care for spiritual and emotional healing will help you remain grounded and discerning.

Nurture Your Spiritual Life

Maybe instead of having doubts about your husband, you have good reason to feel secure. Maybe you feel stronger than you've ever felt before, ready for the full restoration of your marriage. Good!

No matter how you feel right now, remember to nurture

your spiritual life. Follow the apostle Paul's advice in Ephesians 6:13-18 (emphasis added):

> Therefore take up the whole armor of God, that you may be able to withstand in the evil day, and having done all, to stand firm. Stand therefore, having fastened on the belt of *truth*, and having put on the breastplate of *righteousness*, and, as shoes for your feet, having put on the *readiness* given by the gospel of peace. In all circumstances take up the shield of *faith*, with which you can extinguish all the flaming darts of the evil one; and take the helmet of *salvation*, and the sword of the Spirit, which is the *word of God*, *praying* at all times in the Spirit, with all prayer and supplication. To that end, keep alert with all *perseverance*, making supplication for all the saints.

Make use of all the battle resources available to you: God's Word, prayer, support from other believers, and intentional time spent in the presence of the Lord. A steady, consistent spiritual investment will protect you and provide a safe space for you to heal.

Manage the Demands of Life

Debbie checked her calendar on her phone and was surprised to see that she had a parent-teacher conference for her seven-year-old, Ellie, at ten o'clock the next morning. She and her husband, Jerry, had also scheduled a counseling appointment for the same time. Jerry had arranged to take off time from work to be present for the appointment, but Debbie had obviously forgotten to check her calendar. It was too late to call the school and see if she could reschedule the meeting with the teacher, and the counseling appointments were scheduled weeks in advance because of the counselor's very busy practice.

Debbie didn't mention her dilemma to Jerry as they shut off the light to go to bed. Why ruin his night's sleep as well as her own?

Old feelings of inadequacy crept into Debbie's mind as she lay in the silence that surrounded her. Her mental DVD player ran through a series of scenarios, all of them painting her as the bad guy in a messy situation.

Debbie's children, Ellie and Max, had suffered enough during the months leading up to Debbie's confrontation with Jerry. They were too young to understand what was happening, but they certainly understood and felt the constant tension in the house. In fact, the parent-teacher conference was about helping Ellie with her disinterest in school. It was an important appointment that Debbie wanted to keep. But she had also promised Jerry that she would keep up with the joint counseling, no matter how she felt at any given time. Even if she didn't want to go, she had promised that she would stick with their plan and keep the appointments.

Sometime in the middle of the night, Debbie got up and went to the kitchen. She sat at the table with a glass of milk in front of her and thought, *I can't keep up with this . . . this marriage-restoration work and the daily demands of being a mother, a homemaker, a part-time employee, and the daughter of my aging mom. I'm overwhelmed. I'm exhausted. I'm a failure.*

Darkness turned to daylight, and Debbie faced her day.

Does this sound familiar? The details may be different, but

the challenge is the same: Restoring your marriage is a massive task.

You probably notice that I haven't told you what Debbie did. It really doesn't matter. If you identify with Debbie, what matters is what *you* will do when you feel overwhelmed and exhausted from similar demands.

Managing your life now won't be the same as it was prior to your aftershock. There will be times when you need to disappoint others or back out of something you planned to do. The graciousness of others might surprise you. At other times, like Debbie, you will make mistakes because of an overloaded schedule or increased stress. Forgive yourself and try to do better next time.

Debbie had to admit her inability to keep everything in her life perfectly balanced. Then she had to decide whether to try to reschedule one of the meetings and choose the best option.

Like Debbie, you can't be supermom, superwife, or superanything. But you can do the best you can with what you value most. Your relationship with the Lord is obviously right at the top of things you value most, along with your marriage. Certainly, if you have children, they also share that top spot with the Lord and your marriage. Extended family, friends, your church, your job, grocery shopping, laundry, and a host of other relationships and activities all make demands on your life.

Some of your priorities will need to shift to accommodate one that you really do need to follow through on wholeheartedly. Following through wholeheartedly doesn't mean you can't ever reschedule an appointment. But it does mean your commitments regarding recovery deserve time and protection in your life as you make this path *through* pain *toward* renewal.

Immerse Yourself in Recovery

Jesus told His would-be disciples, "Whoever wants to be my disciple must deny themselves and take up their cross daily and follow me" (Luke 9:23, NIV). Following Jesus is an *all-or-nothing proposition*. It's not for the halfhearted or partially committed.

It's exactly the same with marriage, and especially now as you begin this journey toward restoration. You and your husband can turn things around individually, but to restore your marriage successfully as a couple, you'll both have to immerse yourselves in the recovery process. Don't yield to the temptation to just dabble in it.

Gardening is a good illustration of this principle. Seeds will never germinate and grow if you simply dip them in a patch of dirt every so often. The gardener can't give up on a seed if it doesn't push through the soil after a day or two. On the contrary, a seed is transformed into a thriving plant when you plunge it deep into the soil, leave it there for a long time, and allow sunlight and water to produce growth. Growth is a process. Once the seed peeks through the surface of the soil as a green plant, the benefits of God's life-giving plan are evident to the gardener. The seed grew and transformed, becoming what it was designed to be.

The same is true for your marriage. God designed it to be a blessing, and now you both have the opportunity to dig deep into the soil of healing that brings about growth and restoration.

If you only dabble in the recovery process, like the seed that doesn't remain in the soil, your marriage won't become what God designed it to be. You and your husband must throw yourselves into the process lock, stock, and barrel if you want to rekindle the spark of real love and romance. You have to give helpful resources time to breathe life back into your relationship.

God is at work in and through you in ways you can't see. Stay in the soil of recovery, and new life will sprout and grow.

Evaluate Your Support System

Abby's support system included three friends she had known for years: Joan, Hallie, and Leslie. The four women had raised their children at the same time and in the same schools. Their lives overlapped in numerous ways, and they'd grown to love and respect one another.

When Abby discovered that her husband, Carl, was using pornography and growing more and more addicted to it, she confided in these three women. They walked closely with Abby and applauded her courage in confronting Carl. As a result, Carl repented and followed through on all Abby had asked of him. The couple was now meeting with a counselor and making slow progress.

Abby still needed support and her friends' encouragement to stay the course and follow her own plan of recovery. She understood that her friends had spent a huge amount of time with her in person and on the phone. Long talks were a significant part of the support each of them offered. Abby was grateful for their ongoing support.

A year had passed when Joan told Abby that her husband had received a job offer that they needed and wanted to accept. It meant a move. Abby completely understood that Joan could no longer provide the same level of support she had provided the previous year.

After Joan's move, Hallie and Leslie kept meeting and talking with Abby as usual. Their support continued to be invaluable. Abby had many more good days than she used to, but she still experienced painful low times when Hallie and Leslie were necessary lifelines for her in processing her pain.

Then Hallie's mother was diagnosed with cancer, and Hallie became her primary caregiver. Abby again completely understood that Hallie wouldn't be available to support her. Now Hallie needed support *herself* in her role as caregiver to her mother.

Abby shared the loss of the availability of these two close friends with her counselor and her husband and expressed her concerns about leaning too heavily on Leslie. After talking more and praying about it, Abby decided to join a women's support group at her church. The support group wasn't as intimate as her friendships with Joan and Hallie had been, but it helped a great deal.

Leslie was still a big part of Abby's life, so Abby had what she needed to keep healing and growing.

As Abby discovered, life circumstances change for all of us, including for the people in your support system. Your own needs change as well. But you still need significant support as you move ahead with your recovery plan.

From time to time, it would be helpful for you to intentionally evaluate your support system and how it's functioning based on your present and evolving needs. Periodic adjustments or additions may be necessary and even beneficial from season to season of life. Remaining aware and avoiding stagnant or neglected relationships within your support system are key.

Your Inspiration: Believing in God's Amazing Plan

Imagine if you and your husband allow God to make each of you and your marriage totally "new creation[s]" in Christ (2 Corinthians 5:17).

There's no limit to the heights you can reach in your love for one another. When you begin experiencing God's true design for authentic marital intimacy, you won't want to return to the lackluster version of marriage you lived with before. Who wants to eat a rotten apple when you have the option of picking a fresh one from the tree?

Author C. S. Lewis alluded to this same idea when he said, "We are half-hearted creatures, fooling about with [lesser things] when infinite joy is offered us, like an ignorant child who wants to go on making mud pies in a slum because he cannot imagine what is meant by the offer of a holiday at the sea. We are far too easily pleased."[1]

Many couples are overwhelmed as they begin to experience the enormity of God's love. For the first time they're choosing to open their hearts fully. In turn, they're surprised when they experience a newness of love for each other. No longer do they hate to be together in the same room, let alone in the same bed. No longer are they searching the internet for illicit sex or a divorce attorney. Instead, they're looking for a beautiful place to renew their vows.

As you and your husband heal and grow individually and together, you'll be able to create a new vision for your marriage. Your foundation can be built on God's plan of living in a loving relationship with Him and with each other.

As you embrace this vision, know that you'll have good days

and bad days. You'll experience breakthroughs and setbacks. This process is never easy for either spouse. And there will be times when it's downright painful. But I can guarantee that it will also be the most worthwhile project you have ever undertaken.

Remember, God is with you, and He is for you. *He* can see the end even when you can't. He is the visionary Leader who can lead you onward and upward to the final goal. He is good all the time, even when your marriage and life seem to be falling apart. So put your hand in His and keep it there. Trust in Him to make a way for you today and in the future.

The Meaning of Success

You picked up this book because you were experiencing the aftershock of your husband's pornography use and sexual behaviors that were damaging your marriage and causing you a great deal of pain.

You've now received a wealth of information intended to help you heal, grow, and experience personal restoration, as well as the potential restoration of your marriage.

It isn't unusual for women in your situation to feel both overwhelmed and hopeful. You've endured a lot. And now you long for, or are beginning to embrace, success in your recovery. Sometimes we define *success* as "reaching a particular goal, achieving a desired end, and relishing victory over defeat." Success may now be within your reach. You may even be on your way to a finish line, when you and your husband can celebrate the realization of God's design for your marriage.

Like a runner crossing the finish line in a race, you can be glad the hard work is behind you and feel the joy of a race well run. I hope that is true for you. I hope you are, or will be, living on the other side of your arduous work with greater peace and satisfaction.

As that becomes true, the next important focus is to remain healthy and *stay the course*. Life has a way of presenting us with new opportunities for growth and new races to run. Between races, a runner continues to train because a lack of training would make the next race more difficult.

So keep training! If your marriage has been transformed or is moving toward transformation, you're succeeding. You can enjoy the reward of your work as described in this book. Another race will come, but success means that it doesn't have to be the painful or devastating one that this race has been. The next race may involve other challenges of living in a sinful and fallen world. But now you and your husband can face future life hurdles together on the new foundation you're building.

Walking with you on this journey is an honor for me. I'm praying that the following verse will encourage and bless you:

> I bow my knees before the Father, from whom every family in heaven and on earth is named, that according to the riches of his glory he may grant you to be strengthened with power through his Spirit in your inner being, so that Christ may dwell in your hearts through faith—that you, being rooted and grounded in love, may have strength to comprehend with all the saints what is the breadth and length and height and depth, and to know the love of Christ that surpasses knowledge, that you may be filled with all the fullness of God.
>
> EPHESIANS 3:14-19

REFLECTION

> Behold, I am doing a new thing;
> > now it springs forth, do you not perceive it?
> I will make a way in the wilderness
> > and rivers in the desert.
>
> ISAIAH 43:19

QUESTIONS

1. Given where you are today in your recovery process, where do you get your vision and hope from?

2. If your husband isn't yet actively engaging in recovery, what vision can you live toward today that will allow for the possibility of change in your marriage? Do you have vision for yourself and your self-care, too?

3. Think of a couple you and your husband know who have lived through a difficult or devastating time and are experiencing a new and healthier vision for their lives or their marriage. How might recalling their story or visiting with them help you both today?

PRAYER

Lord, help me see a picture in my heart and mind of improvement and renewal. Help me live toward that vision as far as it's up to me. Give hope and vision to my spouse as well. Help us both to grow through the pain and eventually see the fruits of kindness, care, intimacy, and a "banquet" in our friendship and marriage. Help us move forward step by step, with patience and love, into a better vision for our marriage. I will remember to praise You along the way—and when I get there.

ACKNOWLEDGMENTS

WE WOULD LIKE TO ACKNOWLEDGE how *fully* this project has been reliant on others beyond ourselves. The amazing staff and support at Focus on the Family through the years that we (Joann and Geremy) have offered clinical support and ministry to wives has been *much more* than we can adequately note and thank here. To the former clinical and senior directors of the counseling services department at Focus who *believed in* and *spoke life into* this project, we thank you. Specifically, to Tim Sanford (clinical director), whose experience and ability to coach us on clinical issues and writing—you have been an invaluable support. We thank you! To editor Lois Rabey and the entire Focus book publication staff—thank you for your tireless, long-suffering efforts and skills invested in this material to help wives and couples. Getting a book "across the finish line" is no small task. How can we thank you all enough? We can't. *But the Lord can.* May the many unknown, unseen, and

God-ordained supports to this project be thanked and rewarded by the good Lord Himself for the prayerful efforts you put forth to aid us.

With grateful hearts,
Joann and Geremy

APPENDIX A

Sleep Tips: Self-Management of Insomnia

1. Practice relaxation exercises or meditation daily. (This is not the same as taking a nap!) Relax again prior to bedtime.

2. Do nothing in bed, except sleeping (and lovemaking). Do not write, read, watch TV, sew, pay bills, balance your checkbook, argue, discuss, plan, worry, toss and turn, or lie there wide awake. When you catch yourself doing these nonsleep things, get up. Associate your bed with sleep, not work or tension.

3. If you aren't asleep within fifteen minutes after going to bed, get out of bed, go to another room, and engage in some neutral activity (not anything troubling or exciting) until you feel sleepy, at which time you can go back to bed. Don't go to bed simply because it's time to or because you "should," but only because you're tired and ready for sleep. If you feel frustrated and angry because you can't fall sleep, don't keep trying harder and harder.

Turn on the light or go to another room and do something different.

4. Experiment with going to bed later. Start with a half hour later. Many people think they need more sleep than they really do. Rather than lying in bed awake for an hour, stay up an hour longer.

5. Avoid a grim, frantic determination to fall asleep. Getting only a few hours of sleep one night isn't likely to be repeated the next night. You can often make up for lost sleep, so it's not a catastrophe to get little sleep one or even a few nights, unless you worry about it and try too hard to make yourself sleep. Sleep is like relaxation and urination; you can't make it happen. You can only let it happen as you surrender control over it. The harder you try to relax or go to sleep, the more tension and sleeplessness you're likely to experience.

6. If you're lying in bed and realize that you're not likely to fall asleep immediately, you can try to stay awake. This paradoxical technique is called *negative practice*. Trying harder to stay awake is likely to make you feel sleepier, just as trying hard to fall asleep is likely to make you feel wide awake.

7. If you find that your mind is racing and the "motor" won't turn off (such as when you're mentally reviewing the chores and errands you need to do the next few days), get out of bed, find a sheet of paper, and make a list in one column of all the unfinished items of business you're thinking about (such as paying a bill, going to

the dentist, and writing a letter) and opposite each item, make a disposition of it (such as "Will do Thursday," "Will call Joe Monday," "Will text Mary tomorrow before noon"). Then put the list to bed by placing it in a drawer and shutting it as you tell yourself, *Now I've finished with my work, and everything is taken care of.*

8. Reviewing the day's events and planning the next day's activities should be done before (but not immediately before) going to bed. Some people schedule a half hour each day for such sessions. To review the day's events, simply close your eyes and recall each event, from waking in the morning to the present, as if you're watching a videotape of your day. Recall each detail, even the most ordinary.

9. Erratic lifestyles, frequent travel, noisy environments (including aircraft flyovers or spouses who snore), houseguests, fear of the unknown, fear of losing control, and other factors can cause sleep problems. But you can consider several remedies. Making adjustments so you block noise outside your bedroom can help. Anxiety and depression are also frequent causes of insomnia and may require professional therapy. Furthermore, there are certain neurological and respiratory problems that can cause sleep disorders and can only be diagnosed in specially equipped sleep laboratories.

10. People who undergo a work-shift change are likely to experience sleep problems (called *delayed sleep syndrome*). The remedy is to go to sleep later and later until the

sleep-wake cycle normalizes. This may take two or three weeks. (Thus, a shift change every two weeks or even every month makes normalizing the cycle virtually impossible.)

11. Caffeine (in coffee, tea, chocolate, or colas) disturbs sleep, even in people who feel it doesn't. Alcohol helps tense people fall asleep more easily, but the resulting sleep is then fragmented, and premature waking often results. The use of tobacco also disturbs sleep and increases pain symptoms. An overly warm room (higher than 75 degrees) is also likely to make sleep difficult.

12. An occasional sleeping pill may help, but frequent or regular use can result in other problems (e.g., dependency, addiction, and interference with alertness). Always consult your physician before taking this type of medication.

13. Adopt a regular waking time every morning, including weekends, regardless of when you fall asleep the night before. You cannot force yourself to fall asleep, but you can force yourself to wake up. Sleep only until you're refreshed.

14. While conventional wisdom has been to avoid a daytime nap since it's been thought to disturb the rest-wake cycle, more recently some specialists actually encourage short periods of napping to help the body and increase its ability to rest well at night.

15. Regular exercise, especially working out large muscle groups, prepares the body for sleep at night. A brisk walk

APPENDIX A

in the late afternoon or early evening can help, but don't exercise too close to bedtime.

16. Try the old standbys of drinking a glass of warm milk, taking a warm bath or shower, and doing relaxing things a half hour before bedtime. Hunger can disturb sleep, so a light snack might help, but avoid heavy foods.

Copyright © 1999 Joann Condie

APPENDIX B

A Man's Invitation to Recovery

THE FOLLOWING MESSAGE FROM GEREMY KEETON is addressed to your husband. It may be helpful to give it to him after you confront him as described in chapters 6 and 7. Assure your husband that Geremy is a highly qualified therapist who has counseled many men and couples who have struggled with issues similar to the ones you and your husband now face.

From: Geremy Keeton, licensed marriage and family therapist and counselor for men
To: The husband of the reader of *Aftershock*

As much as this book is for women, I want you to know it's very fairly written. It's not aimed at bashing or shaming you, but it does explain what it takes to restore and renew a marriage. You have an opportunity now to change your marriage for the better! You can step up and be the man you were created to be.

Because I've come alongside husbands who've progressed through recovery and now enjoy the fruits of a transformed life and marriage, I can attest to the fact that it's both hard work *and* worth it.

There are few things more beautiful and positively contagious than a redeemed couple! Although this is likely the furthest thing from your view right now, you can have joy and freedom—for yourself and your marriage. Do you want that? It's your turn to show it.

Similarly, it's your wife's turn to face her own recovery and growth in a healthy way. She must respond to her pain in a self-respecting and measured manner as she watches for what you will do. In large part, your actions over time determine how she can proceed and what she'll decide about the marriage.

I'm urging you to recover not only for her sake but also for *yours*. Your most prized possession as a man is your integrity. You can regain this. If you focus solely on your wife and "performing" to regain her and your married lifestyle, then you will almost certainly falter in your recovery. The days when she's most upset with you, the days when she doubts you because she has flashbacks of pain—these are the days you may temporarily throw in the towel and binge on sinful choices and acting out. If she's not happy and this recovery process is so difficult, you may wonder, *What's the point?* You must learn to answer this question with *sincere self-motivation* and your own pursuit of personal integrity and wholeness.

The fact is, an imperfect journey to full recovery is more common than a perfect one. This complicates things. Counselors and nearly any man in an honest recovery group will agree with that. Fortunately, a marriage can usually weather a slip or imperfection if there are sincere and visibly proven efforts to establish full recovery. That's one reason why self-motivation for your own *personal* betterment (underlying a simultaneous battle for your wife's heart) is so essential. It will help sustain you both through the normal peaks and valleys you encounter on the path to restoring your marriage.

Your wife can feel the difference in your motivation and will most often weather any stormy patches that arise if she sees that you're committed to yourself and your recovery in a healthy way. Her ability to tolerate imperfections along the bumpy road to recovery is especially likely if she feels a growing intimacy and emotional availability in how you share honestly with her about your recovery and the actions you're taking.

Come what may for your marriage, the path of personal health and integrity is always best. No one owns your integrity and walk with God but you. You have a life to live—and if you hope to live it with your spouse, then embracing a strong self-motivation and internally driven hunger for healing is the most likely way to accomplish that.

NOTES

INTRODUCTION
1. James W. Pennebaker and Joshua M. Smyth, *Opening Up by Writing It Down: How Expressive Writing Improves Health and Eases Emotional Pain*, 3rd ed. (New York: Guilford Press, 2016).

CHAPTER 2: "CAN I TRUST MY EMOTIONS?"
1. C. S. Lewis, *A Grief Observed* (New York: HarperOne, 1996), 9–10.
2. Lewis, *A Grief Observed*, 3.
3. Annotation by C. H. Spurgeon, *The Salt-Cellars* (New York: A. C. Armstrong and Son, 1889), 62.

CHAPTER 3: "WHAT WAS I THINKING?"
1. Daniel G. Amen, *Change Your Brain, Change Your Life: The Breakthrough Program for Conquering Anxiety, Depression, Anger, and Impulsiveness* (New York: Three Rivers Press, 1998), 60–64.

CHAPTER 5: "WHY DOES HE DO WHAT HE DOES?"
1. Johann Hari, "Everything You Think You Know About Addiction Is Wrong" (TED Talk, TEDGlobalLondon, June 2015), accessed January 28, 2020, https://www.ted.com/talks/johann_hari_everything_you_think_you_know_about_addiction_is_wrong?language=en.
2. Fernando Dangond, "Central Nervous System (CNS) Functions, Parts, and Locations," EMedicineHealth, September 4, 2019, https://www.emedicinehealth.com/anatomy_of_the_central_nervous_system/article_em.htm#central_nervous_system_cns_definition.

3. Neely Tucker, "Daniel Amen Is the Most Popular Psychiatrist in America," *Washington Post*, August 9, 2012, https://www.washingtonpost.com /lifestyle/magazine/daniel-amen-is-the-most-popular-psychiatrist-in -america-to-most-researchers-and-scientists-thats-a-very-bad-thing/2012 /08/07/467ed52c-c540-11e1-8c16-5080b717c13e_story.html.
4. Daniel G. Amen, Kristen Willeumier, and Robert Johnson, "The Clinical Utility of Brain SPECT Imaging in Process Addictions," *Journal of Psychoactive Drugs* 44, no. 1 (2012), 18, https://doi.org/10.1080 /02791072.2012.660101.
5. Amen, "Clinical Utility," 21.

Chapter 8: The Road to Recovery
1. Timothy L. Sanford, *Forgive for Real: Six Steps to Forgiving* (n.p.: LifEdvice, 2019), 119–140. (Sanford's material is presented in an easy-to-read workbook fashion. We recommend using *Forgive for Real* as a separate journal as you work through forgiveness. The six steps presented by Sanford are compatible with the message of *Aftershock*.)
2. Jonathan Daugherty, founder and director of Be Broken Ministries, teaches these concepts in the Gateway to Freedom workshops. For more information, see BeBroken.com and GatewayMen.com.

Chapter 9: Your Sexual Relationship with Your Husband
1. Christopher West, *Fill These Hearts: God, Sex, and the Universal Longing* (New York: Crown Publishing Group, 2012), 138. Regarding sacred sexuality, we have found especially insightful Christopher West's exposition of an influential series of lectures by Pope John Paul II published in *The Theology of the Body: Human Love in the Divine Plan*. To learn more, see the resources and lectures at ChristopherWest.com and CorProject.com.
2. West, *Fill These Hearts*, 138.
3. C. S. Lewis, *Mere Christianity* (New York: Macmillan, 1952), 81.

Chapter 10: Setting Yourself Up for Success
1. C. S. Lewis, *The Weight of Glory* (New York: HarperOne, 1980), 26. Originally preached as a sermon at the Church of St Mary the Virgin, Oxford, England, on June 8, 1942.